VOCA[illegible]Y for the College Bound

BOOK C

2nd Edition
Revised and Expanded

ISBN 978-1-62019-113-2

Prestwick House

Senior Editor: Paul Moliken

Editor: Darlene Gilmore

Cover & Text Design: Larry Knox

Layout: Jeremy Clark

P.O. Box 658 Clayton, Delaware 19938 ŏ www.prestwickhouse.com

Item No. 309270

Table *of* Contents

Strategies for Completing Activities

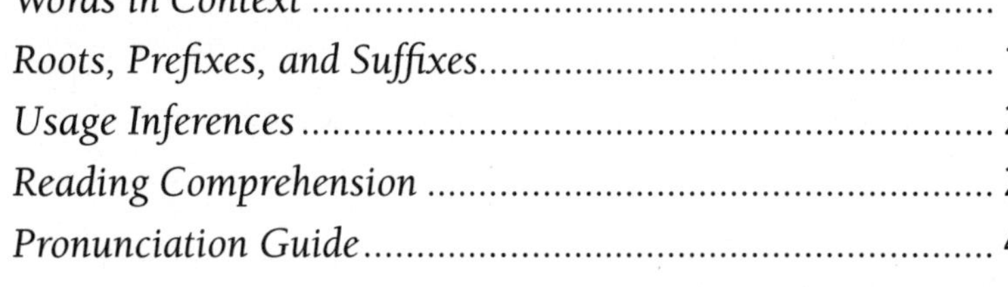

Lessons

Strategies *for* Completing Activities

Words in Context

One way you can make sure that you understand what an unfamiliar word means is to see it used in a sentence and make a guess, an inference, as to its meaning. For example, you probably do not know what the word *theriomorphic* means. Using roots, prefixes, and suffixes will help, as you will see explained below. Read it in the following sentence, though, and you will have another method to arrive at its meaning:

> The drawing on the clay tablet that archaeologists recently discovered depicted a man with antlers and hooves—a *theriomorphic* being—within a ring of fire.

Clues in the sentence enable you to see the context of *theriomorphic*: a primitive drawing showing something not completely human. Therefore, you can infer that *theriomorphic* means "a person who looks like an animal."

Here's another Examples:

> Dawn was a *somnambulist*; on some nights, her family found her in the hall, other times she was discovered in the basement, and once, they found her sitting asleep in the front seat of the car.

After reading the sentence, you should be able to infer that the word *somnambulist* must mean "someone who walks in his or her sleep."

Roots, Prefixes, and Suffixes

To the person interested in words, a knowledge of roots, prefixes, and suffixes turns each new, unfamiliar word into a puzzle. And while it is a sure and lifelong way to build your vocabulary, there are two points to keep in mind.

1. Some words have evolved through usage so that today's definitions are different from the ones you might have inferred from an examination of their roots and/or prefixes. For example, the word *abstruse* contains the prefix *ab–* (away) and the root *trudere* (to thrust) and literally means "to thrust away." But today, the word is used to describe something that is "hard to understand."

2. Occasionally, you may be incorrect about a root. For example, knowing that the root *vin* means "to conquer," you would be correct in concluding that the word *invincible* means "not able to be conquered"; but if you tried to apply that root meaning to the word *vindictive* or *vindicate*, you would miss the actual meaning. So, in analyzing an unfamiliar word, check for other possible roots than the one you first assumed if your inferred meaning doesn't fit the context.

These warnings notwithstanding, a knowledge of roots, prefixes, and suffixes is one of the best ways to build a strong, vital vocabulary.

Usage Inferences

The next method of determining if you understand what a word means is for you to see the word as it might be applied to various situations. Therefore, in a Usage Inference, you need to be able to take the definition you learned into the real world. Remembering the definition and using the word correctly are two different concepts. We supply a series of multiple-choice situations in which you need to figure out the best use of the word.

Let's assume that you learned in a lesson that *specious* means "false or faulty reasoning that seems true" or "an argument that does not stand up to logical reasoning."

Examples:

When or where would making a *specious* argument most likely be challenged?
A. on Friday night asking for the keys to the family car
B. in a jury room debating the guilt of someone on trial
C. with your family deciding on the price of a trip to Hawaii
D. at school trying to convince your friend to go sky diving

While all the answers could be examples of making a specious argument, the one that might cause a problem is B, simply because any faulty argument would most likely be argued against by another juror. Obviously, faulty logic and arguments can be used in A, B, C, and D. After all, saying the wrong thing may prevent getting the keys, spending too much could ruin a trip, and sky diving is dangerous. These three situations, though, are less likely to have flawed logic called into question.

Another key to the correct answer is stated in the question, so make sure that you read that part carefully, as it frequently will narrow down your choices.

Reading Comprehension

Reading questions generally fall into several types.

1. *Identifying the main idea or the author's purpose. In short, the question asks, "What is this selection about?"*

   In some paragraphs, this is easy to spot because there are one or two ideas that leap from the paragraph. In some selections, however, this may be much more difficult, especially if there are convoluted sentences with clauses embedded within clauses. It also may be difficult in those selections in which there are inverted sentences (a sentence with the subject at the end) or elliptical sentences (a sentence in which a word or words are left out). All of these obstacles can be overcome if you take one sentence at a time and put it in your own words.

Consider the following sentence:

> These writers either jot down their thoughts bit by bit, in short, ambiguous, and paradoxical sentences, which apparently mean much more than they say—of this kind of writing Schelling's treatises on natural philosophy are a splendid instance; or else they hold forth with a deluge of words and the most intolerable diffusiveness, as though no end of fuss were necessary to make the reader understand the deep meaning of their sentences, whereas it is some quite simple if not actually trivial idea, examples of which may be found in plenty in the popular works of Fichte, and the philosophical manuals of a hundred other miserable dunces.

But if we edit out some of the words, the main point of this sentence is obvious.

> These writers either jot down their thoughts bit by bit, in short, ambiguous, and paradoxical sentences, which apparently mean much more than they say—of this kind of writing Schelling's treatises on natural philosophy are a splendid instance; or else they hold forth with a deluge of words and the most intolerable diffusiveness, as though [it] end of fuss were necessary to make the reader understand the deep meaning of their sentences, whereas it is son [a] uite simple if not actually trivial idea, examples of which may be found in plenty in the popular works of Fichte, and the philosophical manuals of a hundred other miserable dunces.

While the previous sentence needs only deletions to make it clear, this next one requires major revisions and must be read carefully and put into the reader's own words.

> Some in their discourse desire rather commendation of wit, in being able to hold all arguments, than of judgment, in discerning what is true; as if it were a praise to know what might be said, and not what should be thought.

After studying it, a reader might revise the sentence as follows:

> In their conversations, some people would rather win praise for their wit or style of saying something rather than win praise for their ability to judge between what is true or false—as if it were better to sound good regardless of the quality of thought.

2. *Identifying the stated or inferred meaning. Simply, what is the author stating or suggesting?*

3. *Identifying the tone or mood of the selection or the author's feeling.*

To answer this type of question, look closely at individual words and their connotations. For example, if an author describes one person as stubborn and another as firm, it tells you something of the author's feelings. In the same manner, if the author uses many words with harsh, negative connotations, he is conveying one mood; but if he uses words with milder negative connotations, he may be striving for quite another mood.

Pronunciation Guide

ă	pat	ŏŏ	took
ā	aid, fey, pay	ōō	boot, fruit
â	air, care, wear, ant	ô	ball, haul
ä	father	p	pop
b	bib	r	roar
ch	church	s	miss, sauce, see
d	deed	sh	dish, ship
ĕ	pet, pleasure	t	tight
ē	be, bee, easy, leisure	th	path, thin
f	fast, fife, off, phase, rough	th	this, bathe
g	gag	ŭ	cut, rough
h	hat	û	circle, firm, heard, term, turn, urge, word
ĭ	pit	v	cave, valve, vine
ī	by, guy, pie	w	with
î	dear, deer, fierce, mere	y	yes
j	jury, joke	yōō	abuse, use
k	kiss, clean, quit	z	rose, size, xylophone, zebra
oi	soil, toy	zh	garage, pleasure, vision
ou	cow, out	ə	about, silent, pencil, lemon, circus
ŏ	closet, bother	ər	butter
ō	boat, oh		

Lesson One

1. **adroit** (ə droit′) *adj.* skillful, clever
Everyone knew that he was *adroit* with figures, but he lacked the facility for public speaking.
syn: dexterous, apt *ant:* clumsy, awkward

2. **adulterate** (ə dŭl′ tə rāt) *verb* to make impure; contaminate
adj. impure
The fumes from the automobiles *adulterate* the air.
The police were concerned about all the *adulterated* drugs on the street.
ant: refine, refined

3. **adventitious** (ăd vĕn tĭsh′ əs) *adj.* accidental; nonessential
The scientists announced the breakthrough at a press conference and admitted that it had been an *adventitious* outcome.
syn: incidental

4. **aegis** (ē′ jĭs) *noun* a shield; protection; sponsorship
The candidate felt he had a chance in the election because of the *aegis* of a former officeholder.
syn: backing

5. **aesthetic** (ĕs thĕt′ ĭk) *adj.* pertaining to beauty
The house was a bargain financially, but it lacked any *aesthetic* quality.
syn: artistic

6. **affectation** (ă fĕk tā′ shən) *noun* a phony attitude; pose
John felt that the outspoken Ruth was the only girl there who did not have any *affectations*.
syn: insincerity, sham *ant:* sincerity, genuineness

7. **affinity** (ə fĭn′ ĭ tē) *noun* an attraction to
The young man had an *affinity* for fast cars and easy money.
syn: partiality, fondness *ant:* aversion

8. **affluence** (ă flōō əns) *noun* wealth; richness
Although Paul's family had much *affluence*, he was content to make do without their help.
syn: abundance *ant:* poverty, destitution

9. **agape** (ə gāp′) *adj.* open-mouthed; surprised; agog
Even the judge was *agape* when the witness told the ridiculous story in court.
syn: awestruck

10. **aggrandize** (ə grăn′ dīz) *verb* to enlarge; expand
Much of what they did was not to aid their country, but to *aggrandize* their own positions.
syn: increase, augment, enrich *ant:* decrease, diminish

11. **altruism** (ăl′ trōō ĭz əm) *noun* a concern for others; generosity
Ben's *altruism* was apparent as he stopped at the scene of the accident to offer his assistance.
syn: unselfishness, magnanimity *ant:* selfishness, egoism

12. **ambiguous** (ăm bĭg′ yōō əs) *adj.* open to more than one interpretation
The candidate's *ambiguous* comments tended to confuse the issue even more.
syn: unclear, uncertain, vague *ant:* explicit, definite

13. **amoral** (ā môr′ əl) *adj.* lacking a sense of right and wrong
Although a greedy man, he was not *amoral*; there were some things he would not do for money.

14. **amorphous** (ə môr′ fəs) *adj.* shapeless, formless, vague
The essay was due in two days, but Steve couldn't grasp the topic, which remained *amorphous* in his mind.

15. **animosity** (ăn ə mŏs′ ĭ tē) *noun* hatred
There was a general feeling of *animosity* toward the judge for giving the boys such a harsh sentence.
syn: ill will, hostility *ant:* friendliness, congeniality

Exercise I Words in Context

Fill in the blanks with the correct vocabulary words needed to complete the sentences.

affectations **adroit** **affluence** **adulterated** **affinity**

A. Because he was very ________________ at manipulating stock purchases, his ________________ grew rapidly. Despite his new wealth, however, he did not develop those ________________ usually associated with the nouveau riche. But he did develop an ________________ for life in the fast lane. It was this lifestyle and ________________ drugs that killed him.

amorphous **amoral** **altruistic** **animosity** **aggrandizement**

B. His ________________ toward them had no particular focus; rather, there was an ________________ quality to it. While not a religious man, he disliked churchgoers because he thought them to be ________________. They were not at all ________________; in fact, he thought they were selfish. In those rare instances when they did something for someone, it was done more for self-________________ than from a desire to help others.

adventitious **agape** **aesthetic** **aegis** **ambiguous**

C. Al thought seeing Amy at the party was ________________. Since he was no longer under the ________________ of his uncle, he had lost much of his influence at the museum. As he explained his plan to regain power, Amy stood ________________ in disbelief. She told him in no ________________ terms that she would have absolutely nothing to do with his plan and was interested in art from an ________________ point of view, not as a wedge to gain power.

Exercise II Roots, Prefixes, and Suffixes

Study the entries and answer the questions that follow.

The root *anim* means "feeling," "spirit," "life."
The root *sec/sect* means "cut."
The root *cand* means "white," "shining."
The root *terra* means "earth."
The root *firma* means "solid."
The prefix *uni–* means "one."
The prefix *extra–* means "outside."

1. The literal meaning of *unanimous* is ____________________; if you are filled with strong feelings against someone, you are filled with ____________________. But *animation* is the act of ____________________.

2. Something that is *incandescent* is ____________________; but the word *candid*, meaning "pure, sincere," comes from the same root. What is the word's probable evolution?

3. List other words that use *cand* as a root.

4. The phrase "terra firma" refers to ____________________, but the word ____________________ refers to something from beyond this planet.

5. Give a literal meaning for the following:
   bisect
   intersect
   sector

Exercise III Usage Inferences

Choose the answer that best suits the situation.

1. Which is most likely to be described as *adulterated*?
   A. a mountain stream
   B. a movie on television
   C. a hard fought football game
   D. a fancy dinner party

2. Who is the person most likely to be described as displaying an *affinity* for something?
   A. a first-year English teacher
   B. a person who has 15 cats
   C. a dentist who has retired
   D. a student who hates homework

3. Which directions are the best example of something that is *ambiguous*?
   A. "After you pass the bank, turn left at the first traffic light."
   B. "Remember, this room can never get too cold."
   C. "Wherever you go, remember that rule."
   D. "I want you to stop the fighting right now."

Exercise IV Reading Comprehension

Read the selection and answer the questions.

I went to the woods because I wished to live deliberately, to confront only the essential facts of life, and see if I could not learn what it had to teach, and not, when I came to die, discover that I had not lived. I did not wish to live what was not life, living is so dear; nor did I wish to practice resignation, unless it was quite necessary. I wanted to live deep and suck out all the marrow of life, to live so sturdily and Spartanlike as to put to rout all that was not life, to cut a broad swath and shave close, to drive life into a corner, and reduce it to its lowest terms, and, if it proved to be mean, why then to get the whole and genuine meanness of it, and publish its meanness to the world; or if it were sublime, to know it by experience, and be able to give a true account of it in my next excursion. For most men, it appears to me, are in a strange uncertainty about it, whether it is of the devil or of God and have *somewhat hastily* concluded that it is the chief end of man here to "Glorify God and enjoy him forever."

–Henry David Thoreau

1. In this selection, the author states that his main purpose in going into the woods was to
   A. try to prove the existence of God.
   B. try to disprove the existence of God.
   C. try to find the meaning of life, or at least to find out what life is about.
   D. try to commune with nature.
   E. try to live and die, if necessary, by himself.

2. The author states or implies that
   A. God does not exist.
   B. God does exist, but it cannot be proven empirically.
   C. some men have hastily reached a conclusion about God's existence.
   D. some men have hastily reached a conclusion about the end or meaning of life.
   E. Both C and D are correct.

3. The author's mood may be best described as being very
   A. gloomy.
   B. happy.
   C. depressed.
   D. determined.
   E. irresolute.

4. It is clear that the author believes that
   A. there is a meaning to life.
   B. there is no meaning to life.
   C. one must search on his own for any meaning to life.
   D. the meaning of life is to glorify God.
   E. the Spartans were the first to discover the true meaning of life.

BOOK C

VOCABULARY *for the* College Bound

Lesson Two

1. **antipathy** (ăn tĭp´ə thē) *noun* an intense dislike
   So great was her feeling of *antipathy* that she was afraid it showed in her face.
   syn: aversion *ant:* affinity

2. **antithesis** (ăn tĭth´ ĭ sĭs) *noun* an exact opposite; an opposite extreme
   Love is the *antithesis* of hate.

3. **badinage** (băd ən äzh´) *noun* playful, teasing talk
   verb to banter; to tease with playful talk
   Although it started out as *badinage*, it quickly escalated to cutting insults.

4. **banal** (bə näl´) *adj.* common, ordinary
   His *banal* remarks quickly bored the entire class.
   syn: trivial, insipid *ant:* original, fresh

5. **baroque** (bə rōk´) *adj.* overly decorated
   The new dance club had a great light show; the *baroque* furnishings seemed right in place.
   syn: ornate *ant:* simple

6. **bauble** (bô´ bəl) *noun* a showy but useless thing
   John had to find some kind of *bauble* to give Mary for Christmas.
   syn: trinket

7. **bedlam** (bĕd´ ləm) *noun* a noisy uproar; a scene of wild confusion
   The concert hall was sheer *bedlam* until the rock star appeared.

8. **beguile** (bĭ gīl´) *verb* to deceive; charm; enchant
   In *Gone with the Wind*, Scarlett O'Hara tried to *beguile* all the eligible men she met.

9. **besiege** (bĭ sēj´) *verb* to overwhelm; to surround and attack
   Congressmen were *besieged* with phone calls during the controversial hearings.

10. **besmirch** (bĭ smûrch´) *verb* to make dirty; stain
    My ex-best friend tried to *besmirch* my reputation with her vicious gossip.
    syn: soil, sully, smear *ant:* cleanse

11. **bestial** (bĕs´ chəl) *adj.* savage, brutal
    He took a *bestial* delight in tormenting the captive slaves.
    syn: brutish, vile, cruel *ant:* humane, kind

12. **bilious** (bĭl′ yəs) *adj.* bad tempered; cross
No one could stand being in the same room with Sam when he was in a *bilious* mood.
syn: grouchy, cantankerous *ant:* pleasant

13. **blanch** (blănch) *verb* to whiten, to make pale
Sue's face *blanched* visibly when she saw the charred remains of what had been her home.

14. **bland** (blănd) *adj.* mild, tasteless, dull
His *bland* manner had a calming effect on the children.
syn: benign, mellow *ant:* exciting, thrilling

15. **blandishment** (blăn′ dĭsh mənt) *noun* flattery
The salesman's smooth *blandishments* did not convince the customer to buy the expensive clothing.

Exercise I Words in Context

Fill in the blanks with the correct vocabulary words needed to complete the sentences.

besieged **bedlam** **antithesis** **badinage**

A. The party was in ________________ when Ed and Lisa arrived. It was the complete ________________ of the sedate cocktail party they had just left where the ________________ of the guests was most pleasant. Now, the loud music and even louder talk made them feel ________________, so they left at the first opportunity.

antipathy **banal** **bland** **besmirch** **baroque**

B. The decorator had a(n) ________________ for anything ________________. He preferred subtle colors and earth tones to convey his message. Emily, however, felt that his ideas were ________________, and she wanted something more spectacular. She did not want to ________________ his reputation, but in the end, she did so by telling all of her friends how ________________ she felt his ideas were.

bestial **blanched** **blandishments** **bauble** **bilious** **beguile**

C. The ________________ that Mark gave to Elizabeth was supposed to ________________ her, but instead, it made her ________________. She knew what it had cost, and his face ________________ visibly when she called him a cheapskate. None of Mark's further ________________ could change her mind. Finally, an outraged Mark said that she was acting in a ________________ manner.

Exercise II Roots, Prefixes, and Suffixes

Study the entries and answer the questions that follow.

The root *apt* means "fit."
The root *aster/astr* means "star."
The root *bas* means "low."
The prefix *dis–* means "bad."
The prefix *de–* means "reduce."
The prefix *in–* means "not."

1. The word *disaster* is made from the root *aster,* and the prefix *dis–* means "misfortune or calamity." Explain how we get the word *distaster* from these elements.

2. An *aptitude* for a job implies a __________________, however an *ineptitude* indicates an __________________.

3. Literally, to *debase* someone is to __________________ them. A five-letter word beginning with an "a" and meaning much the same thing is __________________.

4. List as many words as you can think of that contain the roots *aster/astr,* and *bas.*

Exercise III Usage Inferences

Choose the answer that best suits the situation.

1. Which term is the best example of the *antithesis* of freedom?
   A. liberty
   B. bondage
   C. friendship
   D. communism

2. Which one of the following could be described as a *bauble*?
   A. a judge's oak gavel
   B. a pro golfer's favorite putter
   C. a dog's flea collar
   D. a baseball player's gold earring

3. Which situation would most likely cause someone to use the word *bestial*?
   A. a violent outburst during a trial
   B. the rowdy celebration after a championship
   C. a car accident
   D. the beating of a prisoner

Exercise IV Reading Comprehension

Read the selection and answer the questions.

It was about that time I conceived the bold and arduous project of arriving at moral perfection. I wished to live without committing any fault at any time; I would conquer all that either natural inclination, custom, or company might lead me into. As I knew, or thought I knew, what was right and wrong, I did not see why I might not always do the one and avoid the other. But I soon found I had undertaken a task of more difficulty than I had imagined. While my care was employed in guarding against one fault, I was often surprised by another; habit took the advantage of inattention; inclination was sometimes too strong for reason. I concluded, at length, that the mere speculative conviction that it was in our interest to be completely virtuous was not sufficient to prevent our slipping; and that the contrary habits must be broken, and good ones acquired and established, before we can have any dependence on a steady, uniform rectitude of conduct. For this purpose I therefore contrived the following method.

In the various enumerations of the moral virtues I had met within my reading, I found the catalog more or less numerous, as different writers included more or fewer ideas under the same name. Temperance, for example, was by some confined to eating and drinking, while by others it was extended to mean the moderating of every other pleasure, appetite, inclination, or passion, bodily or mental, even to our avarice and ambition. I proposed to myself, for the sake of clearness, to use rather more names, with fewer ideas annexed to each, than a few names with more ideas; and I included under thirteen names of virtues all that at that time occurred to me as necessary or desirable, and annexed to each a short precept, which fully expressed the extent I gave to its meaning.

–Benjamin Franklin

1. The plan that this author is expounding is one which is calculated to
   A. improve his physical health.
   B. improve his mental health.
   C. enrich him in worldly goods.
   D. bring him closer to God.
   E. help him eradicate his vices and improve his virtues.

2. The author states or implies that
   A. cleanliness is next to Godliness.
   B. while it is easy to know what is right, it is harder to do what is right.
   C. in setting up his plan, he drew on the works of other writers.
   D. Both B and C are correct.
   E. A, B, and C are correct.

3. The author appears to be a man who is
   A. something of a scatterbrain.
   B. very organized and logical.
   C. designing an elaborate joke.
   D. not very happy with his life.
   E. often accused of drinking too much.

4. The best title for this selection would be
   A. Conquering Natural Inclinations.
   B. Arriving at Moral Perfection.
   C. Enumerating Moral Virtues.
   D. Moderating Pleasures.
   E. Speculative Conviction and Virtue.

Lesson Three

1. **bombast** (bäm′ băst) *noun* impressive but meaningless language
Please, professor, no more *bombast*; just give me the facts.

2. **bona fide** (bō′ nə fīd) *adj.* in good faith
We made a *bona fide* offer for the property.
syn: legitimate, genuine *ant:* fraudulent, phony

3. **boor** (bo͝or) *noun* a rude or impolite person
My brother was acting like a *boor*.
syn: buffoon, clown *ant:* sophisticate

4. **bovine** (bō′ vīn) *adj.* pertaining to cows or cattle
The critic described the large figures in the painting as *bovine*.

5. **bowdlerize** (bōd′ lər īz) *verb* to remove offensive passages of a play, novel, etc.
If the editors *bowdlerize* much more of the book, there won't be anything left to read.
syn: censor

6. **brevity** (brĕv′ ĭ tē) *noun* briefness; a short duration
The *brevity* of the candidate's speech surprised everyone.
syn: terseness, conciseness *ant:* long-windedness

7. **bucolic** (byo͞o kŏl′ ĭk) *adj.* pertaining to the countryside; rural, rustic
Jim wanted to find an old inn in a *bucolic* setting in which to have lunch.
syn: pastoral

8. **cajole** (kə jōl′) *verb* to coax, persuade, wheedle
Tim tried to *cajole* his parents into letting him use the new car.

9. **callow** (kă′ lō) *adj.* young and inexperienced
Although he was not the typical *callow* youth, he was not as experienced as he pretended.
syn: immature *ant:* mature, sophisticated

10. **carcinogen** (kär sĭn′ ə jən) *noun* a substance that causes cancer
It is widely believed that nicotine is a *carcinogen*.

11. **carnal** (kär′ nəl) *adj.* sensual, sexual
Even though Evelyn didn't understand the painting, she knew it had a *carnal* feeling about it.
syn: erotic, voluptuous *ant:* chaste, modest

12. **carrion** (kăr′ ē ən) *noun* decaying flesh
The vultures circling in the sky led the border patrol to the *carrion* they had been seeking since the report of the disaster.

13. **cataclysm** (kăt′ ə klĭz əm) *noun* a violent change
The earthquake in Mexico was a *cataclysm* that no one could have foreseen.
syn: disaster, catastrophe *ant:* triumph, boon

14. **cataract** (kăt′ ə răkt) *noun* a large waterfall; an abnormality of the eye
Because of the *cataracts* in that part of the river, you can't put a canoe in the water.
My grandmother had to have a *cataract* surgically removed from her eye.

15. **caveat** (kă′ vē ät) *noun* a warning
John did not heed that old *caveat* about swimming alone because he had such confidence in his own ability.

Exercise I Words in Context

Fill in the blanks with the correct vocabulary words needed to complete the sentences.

bovine **bombastic** **carnal** **cajoled**

A. The parents objected to the ________________ aspects of the movie, not to the language.

B. When the professor said that all the well-fed people in his family picture had a ________________ appearance, Mark became very angry. He wanted to rush in and call the professor a ________________ old windbag, but Joan ________________ him into calming down and sleeping on it before he took any action.

brevity **bona fide** **caveat** **callow**

C. The ________________ real estate salesman had no idea that the offer was ________________. He felt that the ________________ of the negotiations indicated that something was wrong. He kept thinking of the old ________________ "Buyer Beware."

carrion **cataract** **carcinogen** **bowdlerized** **boor** **cataclysm** **bucolic**

D. Upon retiring to the __________ life of the gentleman farmer, Jim was seen by his wife as something of a __________. She believed that only a __________ would shock him into his old self. It was only after the doctor told her that Jim was slowly losing his vision and that a __________ operation was necessary that she understood why he had been acting as he had.

E. Jeff discovered that one of the bodies had been taken to the medical examiner's office to determine if death had been caused by a __________, but he learned that the remaining bodies had been left as __________ for the vultures. That evening, Jeff wrote a lengthy and very gory account of what he learned and gave it to his editor. When it appeared in the paper the next day, though, it was so __________ he barely recognized his own story.

Exercise II Roots, Prefixes, and Suffixes

Study the entries and answer the questions that follow.

The root *cap/capt* means "take" "hold."
The suffix *–ive* means "relating to."
The root *capit* means "head."
The root *ced/cess* means "yield," "go."
The prefix *de–* means "off."
The prefix *pro–* means "forward."
The prefix *re–* means "back."
The prefix *ante–* means "before."

1. Literally the *capital* of a state is the __________; and if someone is *decapitated*, he is __________.

2. Give the literal meaning of the following:
   procession
   recession
   antecedent
   cessation

3. Someone who is able to take hold is said to be __________, but a *capacious* vessel would be one that __________.

Exercise III Usage Inferences

Choose the answer that best suits the situation.

1. Which scene is the most likely to be described as *bucolic*?
   A. a young man fishing from an ocean pier
   B. a car chase through the streets of Chicago
   C. an astronomer looking through his telescope
   D. five cows grazing in a pasture

2. Where would you be most likely to find *carrion*?
   A. along the side of a country road
   B. in an expensive French restaurant
   C. at a fancy dress ball
   D. in the waiting room of a hospital

3. Which is most likely to be associated with *cataracts*?
   A. Mount Rushmore
   B. the Grand Canyon
   C. the moon
   D. the Great Wall of China

4. Where are you most likely to find a *caveat*?
   A. in a book about hiking in the mountains
   B. in a birthday card
   C. in a fortune cookie
   D. in a speech commemorating Independence Day

Exercise IV Reading Comprehension

Read the selection and answer the questions.

The old fable covers a doctrine ever new and sublime; that there is One Man, present to all particular men only partially, or through one faculty; and that you must take the whole society to find the whole man. Man is not a farmer, or a professor, or an engineer, but he is all. Man is priest, and scholar, and statesman, and producer, and soldier. In the *divided* or social state these functions are parceled out to individuals, each of whom aims to do his stint of the joint work, whilst each other performs his. The fable implies that the individual, to possess himself, must sometimes return from his own labor to embrace all the other laborers. But, unfortunately, this original unit, this fountain of power, has been so distributed to multitudes, has been so minutely subdivided and peddled out, that it is spilled into drops, and cannot be gathered. The state of society is one in which the members have suffered amputation from the trunk, and strut about so many walking monsters, a good finger, a neck, a stomach, an elbow, but never a man.

Man is thus metamorphosed into a thing, into many things. The planter, who is Man sent out into the field to gather food, is seldom cheered by any idea of the true dignity of his ministry. He sees his bushel and his cart, and nothing beyond, and sinks into the farmer, instead of Man on the Farm. The tradesman scarcely ever gives an ideal worth to his work, but is ridden by the routine of his craft, and the soul is subject to dollars. The priest becomes a form; the attorney a statute book; the mechanic a machine; the sailor a rope of the ship.

–Ralph Waldo Emerson

1. In this selection, the author
   A. appears to regret that men see themselves in terms of their jobs.
   B. appears to applaud the specialization of labor.
   C. ridicules man, his society, and his world.
   D. is happy because workers have been released from drudgery.
   E. states that mechanics now do what man used to do.

2. The main idea in this selection is that
   A. craftsmen should perform their work for the love of the work, not money.
   B. whatever your occupation, high or low, be proud of it.
   C. man is an insignificant creature.
   D. man has been fragmented and identifies himself by his occupation rather than by his integrated essence.
   E. the state of society has been metamorphosed, and a new and better order is coming.

3. The author states or implies that
   A. craftsmen have lost the joy in their work and now work mainly for money.
   B. Man must aspire to greatness if he is to be great.
   C. Man can do nothing on his own without God's help.
   D. Both A and B are correct.
   E. A, B, and C are correct.

4. Toward the end of the first paragraph, the author compares the state of society to
   A. a machine.
   B. a craftsman.
   C. an insect.
   D. a cart without a horse.
   E. a human body.

Lesson Four

1. **celibate** (sĕl′ ə bĭt) *adj.* abstaining from sex
   In that religion, the priests take vows to remain impoverished and *celibate*.

2. **censure** (sĕn′ shər) *verb* to criticize sharply
   Congress voted to *censure* the young congressman because of his unethical behavior.
   syn: blame, condemn, reproach *ant:* praise, applaud

3. **cessation** (sĕ sā′ shən) *noun* a stopping; discontinuance
   Although there was a *cessation* in the hostilities, no one doubted that the battle would resume the next day.
   syn: pause, ceasing *ant:* beginning, commencement

4. **chaff** (chăf) *noun* worthless matter
   "Give me just the facts," the professor said. "Separate the wheat from the *chaff*."

5. **chagrin** (shə grĭn′) *noun* embarrassment; a complete loss of courage
   Joanne had never felt such *chagrin* as the time when she fell into the mud puddle in front of her fiancée's family.

6. **chimerical** (kə mĕr′ ĭ kəl) *adj.* imaginary; fantastic
   Although they laughed at his plans and called them *chimerical*, later events proved him to be a visionary.
   syn: absurd, illusionary *ant:* practical

7. **coalesce** (kō ə lĕs′) *verb* to blend, merge
   The anti-war group was made up of such different personalities that it took months before they could *coalesce* into a group that had some power.
   syn: mix, unite, combine *ant:* separate, divide

8. **debacle** (dĭ bä′ kəl) *noun* a complete failure; total collapse
   After reading the reviews, the actors knew the play was a *debacle* and would close in one night.
   syn: disaster, calamity *ant:* success, triumph

9. **debauchery** (dĭ bôch′ ə rē) *noun* corruption; self-indulgence
   He lived a life sunk in sin and *debauchery*.
   syn: excess, dissipation

10. **deference** (dĕf′ ə rəns) *noun* respect; consideration
In *deference* to the young widow, we moved quietly aside and allowed her to leave first.
syn: regard, honor *ant:* contempt

11. **defile** (dĭ fīl′) *verb* to pollute, corrupt
The oil spill was of concern to the populace because it was bound to *defile* the streams and rivers for miles around.

12. **deign** (dān) *verb* to lower oneself before an inferior
"After what she did to me, I would not *deign* to say hello to her," Mary said to Joe about her former best friend.
syn: stoop, condescend

13. **delineate** (dĭ lĭn′ ē āt) *verb* to describe, depict
The politician went on to *delineate* his proposal on disarmament in greater detail.

14. **demeanor** (dĭ mē′ nər) *noun* the behavior; manner of conducting oneself
Believe me, his shy *demeanor* is just an act; he is really quite wild.
syn: deportment

15. **denouement** (dā nōō mä′) *noun* an outcome, result
Hazel prided herself on being able to solve mysteries, but the story she was reading was elusive, and the *denouement* didn't come until the final page.
syn: conclusion

Exercise I Words in Context

Fill in the blanks with the correct vocabulary words needed to complete the sentences.

cessation **chimerical** **debacle** **chagrined**

A. The president called for a ________________ of hostilities between the two warring countries, but his appeal was ignored, and as a result, he was quite ________________.

B. Many of his opponents called it a ________________ notion and predicted that it would end in a ________________ that would take years to recover from.

coalesce **demeanor** **defiling** **denouement** **censure** **chaff**

C. In the ________________, Holmes explained to Watson that he was able to infer very much from the ________________ of the redheaded man. Then, after a little investigation, the clues began to ________________, and a solution became apparent.

D. During the hearings, the senator was accused of ________________ the reputation of many innocent men; hence, they voted to ________________ him. One of his critics said, "The senator never evaluated his information; if he had separated the important from the ________________, he would never have said half the things he did."

delineate **deference** **deign** **debauchery** **celibacy**

E. The young priest, who had taken vows of poverty and ________________, was sent to work in the poorest section of the city. At first, he had problems dealing with the ________________ around him and would not ________________ to talk with the people whose wasted lives he saw. He found it difficult to ________________ his feelings to his superiors, for whom he demonstrated great ________________. After many months, when he was still unable to work out his feelings, he was transferred to another position.

Exercise II Roots, Prefixes, and Suffixes

Study the entries and answer the questions that follow.

The root *celer* means "swift."
The root *cord* means "heart."
The root *clin* means "lean" "bend."
The root *curr/curs* means "run."
The prefix *in–* means "into."
The prefix *de–* means "down."
The prefix *ad–* means "towards"; before *c*, it becomes *ac*.

1. Someone who acts with *celerity* is acting ________________, and the word *accelerate* means ________________________, but if you slow down, you________________.

2. An *inclination* is a ________________, and another word for a sloping hill is an ________________.

3. List as many words as you can think of that contain the root *cord*.

4. A *cursory* reading would be one that is done ________________.

5. List as many words as you can think of that contain the root *curr/curs* and give a literal meaning for each.

Exercise III Usage Inferences

Choose the answer that best suits the situation.

1. Who is the most likely to be *censured*?
   A. a soccer player who never scores a goal
   B. a dentist who causes considerable pain
   C. a rude waitress
   D. a judge who takes a bribe

2. Which of the following situations is the best example of being *chagrined*?
   A. A wagon train gets through a snowstorm to its destination.
   B. A rocket launch is postponed because of computer problems.
   C. A fighter comes in second in a boxing tournament.
   D. A driver is forced off of the road by a truck.

Exercise IV Reading Comprehension

Read the selection and answer the questions.

In this distribution of functions the scholar is the delegated intellect. In the right state he is Man Thinking. In the degenerate state, when the victim of society, he tends to become a mere thinker, or still worse, the parrot of other men's thinking. Let us see him in his school, and consider him in reference to the main influences he receives.

The first in time and the first in importance of the influences upon the mind is that of nature. Every day, the sun; and, after sunset, night and her stars. Ever the winds blow; ever the grass grows. Every day, men and women, conversing, beholding and beholden. The scholar is he of all men whom this spectacle most engages. He must settle its value in his mind. What is nature to him? There is never a beginning, there is never an end, to the inexplicable continuity of this web of God, but always circular power returning into itself. Therein it resembles his own spirit, whose beginning, whose ending, he never can find—so entire, so boundless. Nature hastens to render account of herself to the mind. Classification begins. To the young mind everything is individual, stands by itself. By and by, it finds how to join two things and see in them one nature; then three, then three thousand; and so, tyrannized over by its own unifying instinct, it goes on tying things together, diminishing anomalies, discovering roots running underground whereby contrary and remote things cohere and flower out from one stem. It presently learns that since the dawn of history there has been a constant accumulation and classifying of facts. But what is classification but the perceiving that these objects are not chaotic, and are not foreign, but have a law which is also a law of the human mind? The astronomer discovers that geometry, a pure abstraction of the human mind, is the measure of planetary motion. The chemist finds proportions and intelligible method throughout matter; and science is nothing but the finding of analogy, identity, in the most remote parts.

–Ralph Waldo Emerson

1. This selection was probably taken from Emerson's work entitled
   A. "Self Reliance."
   B. "Nature."
   C. "Common Sense."
   D. "The American Scholar."
   E. "Character."

2. At his best, the scholar is
   A. the delegated intellect.
   B. the most virtuous person.
   C. the man who thinks.
   D. the man who reads and repeats what he reads.
   E. Both A and B are correct.

3. The most important influence on the scholar is
   A. what he reads.
   B. what he learns from others.
   C. what he learns from nature.
   D. what he believes.
   E. Both C and D are correct.

4. For Emerson, nature is
   A. the first influence on the scholar.
   B. one with man.
   C. open to all kinds of classifications because nature is not chaotic.
   D. linked with both man and God.
   E. All of the above are correct.

VOCABULARY for the College Bound

Lesson Five

1. **deride** (dĭ rīd´) *verb* to ridicule, mock
The professor was unpopular because he *derided* his students if they made a mistake.
syn: scorn *ant:* praise

2. **desiccated** (dĕs´ ĭ kāt əd) *adj.* dried up
When she opened the old Bible, one yellow, *desiccated* rose fell to the floor.

3. **despicable** (də spĭ´ kə bəl) *adj.* contemptible, hateful
Only a *despicable* cad would behave so horribly.
syn: vile, base *ant:* laudable, worthy

4. **desultory** (dĕ´ səl tôr ē) *adj.* wandering from subject to subject
He gave his talk in such a *desultory* fashion that it was hard to understand.
syn: disconnected, rambling

5. **deviate** (dē´ vē āt) *verb* to turn aside
Sometimes, it's better to *deviate* from the truth rather than hurt someone's feelings.
syn: digress, stray

6. **diadem** (dī´ ə dem) *noun* a crown
Peter referred to his wife's blonde hair as her golden *diadem*.

7. **diaphanous** (dī ăf´ ə nəs) *adj.* very sheer and light
The *diaphanous* gown was beautiful, but Gloria wasn't sure she had the nerve to wear it.
syn: transparent, gossamer *ant:* opaque

8. **dichotomy** (dī kot´ ə mē) *noun* a division into two parts
While most of us see a *dichotomy* between the real and the unreal, some people contend that there is an overlapping.

9. **ebullient** (ĭ bŭl´ yənt) *adj.* enthusiastic
The *ebullient* crowd cheered as the royal family appeared.
syn: exuberant, lively *ant:* dejected, dispirited

10. **eclectic** (ĕ klĕk´ tĭk) *adj.* choosing from various sources
The room was furnished in an *eclectic* manner, but it all came together very well.
syn: discriminating, selective, catholic *ant:* narrow

11. **edify** (ĕd´ ə fī) *verb* to improve someone morally
The sermon was meant to *edify* the congregation.

12. **effete** (ĕ fēt′) *adj.* worn out; barren
The business model that had excited so many people now seemed irrelevant and *effete*.
syn: exhausted, spent, sterile *ant:* vital, vigorous

13. **egregious** (ĭ grē′ jəs) *adj.* remarkably bad; outrageous
His remark was so *egregious* that it shocked everyone at the party.
syn: flagrant, gross *ant:* moderate

14. **elegy** (ĕl′ ə jē) *noun* a sad or mournful poem
Although she liked all poetry, she particularly liked those *elegies* that made her cry.

15. **elicit** (ĭ lĭs′ ĭt) *verb* to draw forth; call forth
The attorney tried to *elicit* a response from his client, but the man remained mute.

Exercise I Words in Context

Fill in the blanks with the correct vocabulary words needed to complete the sentences.

ebullient **dichotomy** **diadem** **diaphanous** **egregious**

A. At her coronation, the new queen's ________________ dress and golden ________________ met with the ________________ approval of the crowd. It seemed to prove that the ________________ between the rich and the poor did not affect the royal family. In only one generation, however, the ________________ behavior of her children and their spouses turned the people against the monarchy.

elegy **edifying** **effete** **eclectic** **elicited**

B. The ________________ had made Sally cry because it ________________ all of the old memories of her grandmother. Sally's grandmother had been old and ________________, but Sally could remember the interesting, ________________ person she had been; she was a person who was truly ________________ to all who had known her.

deviate **despicable** **deride** **desultory** **desiccated**

C. John felt that it would be fun to ________________ the ________________ old man because the man would be unable to defend himself. John's friends felt his behavior was so ________________ that they walked out and left without him.

D. John's father was agitated. Since his return John had behaved in a ________________ manner, never quite giving anything his full attention. His father, on the other hand, was goal-oriented. He would chart a course and never ________________ from it.

Exercise II Roots, Prefixes, and Suffixes

Study the entries and answer the questions that follow.

The root *derm* means "skin."
The root *di* means "day."
The root *dign* means "worthy."
The root *domin* means "lord" "master."
The root *myco* means "mushroom" or "fungus."
The root *ann* means "year."
The root *domi* means "home."
The prefix *in–* means "not."
The prefix *con–* means "together."

1. If you have *dermatomycosis*, you have ________________ and, of course, would find this on your ________________.

2. You would most likely see a *diurnal* animal ________________, as opposed to a *nocturnal* animal, which you would see ________________.

3. Someone considered very worthy is said to be a ________________. On the other hand, if you treat someone as unworthy, you are committing an ________________ against him; and this is likely to give rise to a feeling of ________________ in him.

4. The expression *Anno Domini* means ________________. One who is *dominant* is literally ________________, and where he lives is his ________________, unless he lives in a building in which others also own apartments. This building is called a ________________.

Exercise III Usage Inferences

Choose the answer that best suits the situation.

1. Which is the best example of something being *derided* in a newspaper?
   A. an advertisement for a car dealership
   B. an editorial supporting a higher drinking age
   C. a cartoon showing a politician falling down
   D. a report of an apartment fire

2. Where are you most likely to read that something has been *desiccated*?
   A. in a description of a waterfall in a travel magazine
   B. in a book about making raisins
   C. in the description of a monument to western pioneers
   D. in a magazine about sports

3. Which character in a play is most likely to wear a *diaphanous* costume?
   A. a good fairy who appears in a dream
   B. a warrior who is getting ready for battle
   C. a king getting ready for bed
   D. a wizard casting a spell

4. Which action is most likely to be called an *egregious* error in judgment?
   A. A cook forgets to put salt in the stew.
   B. A painter drips paint on the floor.
   C. An airplane pilot takes off an hour late because of bad weather.
   D. A bridge builder uses too much sand in the concrete that he mixes.

Exercise IV Reading Comprehension

Read the selection and answer the questions.

When we two were born, this country was still dominated by a selected class bred by political marriages. The commercial class had not then completed the first twenty-five years of its new share of political power; and it was, itself, selected by money qualification, and bred, if not by political marriage, at least by pretty rigorous class marriage. Today the aristocracy and plutocracy still furnish the figureheads of politics, but they are now dependent on the votes of the promiscuously bred masses. And this, if you please, at the very moment when the political problem, having suddenly ceased to mean an occasional meaningless prosecution of dynastic wars, has become the industrial reorganization of Britain, the construction of a practically international Commonwealth, and the partition of the whole of Africa and perhaps the whole of Asia by the civilized Powers. Can you believe that the people whose conceptions of society and conduct, whose power of attention and scope of interest, are measured by the British theatre as you know it today, can either handle this colossal task themselves, or understand and support the sort of mind and character that is (at least comparatively) capable of handling it? For remember: when our voters are in the pit and gallery they are also in the polling booth. We are all now under what Burke called "the hoofs of the swinish multitude." Burke's language gave great offense because the implied exceptions to its universal application made it a class insult; and it certainly was not for the pot to call the kettle black.

–George Bernard Shaw

1. The author opens by stating or implying that when he was born, Britain was governed by
   A. wealthy, middle-class storekeepers.
   B. wealthy aristocrats.
   C. poor but honest tradesmen.
   D. safe and predictable politicians.
   E. voters from the lower classes.

2. He then states or implies that today Britain is governed by
   A. wealthy aristocrats elected by the poor people.
   B. poor people elected by the poor people.
   C. the middle class shop keepers elected by the commercial classes.
   D. Both B and C are correct.
   E. A, B, and C are correct.

3. At this point, the political problems facing Britain are
   A. industrial reorganization.
   B. building the Commonwealth.
   C. dividing the underdeveloped continents of Asia and Africa with other European powers.
   D. Both A and B are correct.
   E. All of the above are correct.

4. The author appears to believe that the present political establishment
   A. has been well trained for its job.
   B. is not up to the job in front of it.
   C. means well but lacks experience.
   D. is the best available.
   E. should be left alone so it can get on with the job.

VOCABULARY for the College Bound

Lesson Six

1. **elixir** (ĭ lĭk′ sər) *noun* a supposed remedy for all ailments
The *elixir* that Mrs. Higgins used for colds was a secret that had been handed down in her family from generation to generation.
syn: medicine, panacea

2. **elucidate** (ĭ lo͞o′ sĭ dāt) *verb* to make clear
To *elucidate* and bolster his argument, he drew a large chart on the board.
syn: explain, clarify *ant:* obscure

3. **emanate** (ĕm′ ə nāt) *verb* to come forth; send forth
She tried to control her anger, but harsh words began to *emanate* from her lips.
syn: rise, emerge

4. **emendation** (ē men dā′ shən) *noun* a correction
The last edition of the book contains many *emendations*.

5. **empathy** (ĕm′ pə thē) *noun* an understanding of another's feelings
As Laurie's face became redder by the minute, I felt a certain *empathy* for her.

6. **empirical** (ĕm pîr′ ĭ kəl) *adj.* based on evidence rather than theory
He was the first to present *empirical* data to support the argument that smoking is harmful.
syn: observable *ant:* theoretical

7. **endemic** (ĕn dĕm′ ĭk) *adj.* confined to a particular country or area
Once the disease had been *endemic* to Africa, but now it is becoming a worldwide epidemic.

8. **enervate** (ĕn′ ər vāt) *verb* to weaken
Because the hot, humid weather *enervated* the boys, they were content to sit in the shade.
syn: devitalize, exhaust *ant:* energize, strengthen

9. **ennui** (än wē′) *noun* boredom; a weariness resulting from a lack of interest
Because the speaker sensed a feeling of *ennui* settling over the audience, he told a joke.
ant: excitement, interest

10. **ephemeral** (ĭ fĕm′ ər əl) *adj.* lasting only a brief time; short-lived
The celebrity who doesn't realize that fame is *ephemeral* is in for a rude awakening when people no longer know or care who the person is.
syn: transient, fleeting *ant:* permanent

11. **epitome** (ĭ pĭt′ ə mē) *noun* a typical example; a condensed account
As he saw to the comfort of his guests, he was the *epitome* of Southern hospitality.
syn: representative, summary

12. **ergo** (ĕr′ gō) *conjunction* therefore
I am broke; *ergo*, I can't pay the rent this week.
syn: consequently, hence

13. **erotic** (ĭ rŏt′ ĭk) *adj.* pertaining to sexual love
The statues in the museum were thought to be too *erotic* to allow young children to view them.

14. **eschew** (ĕs chōō′) *verb* to keep away from; avoid; shun
Embrace virtue and *eschew* sin was the theme of the minister's sermon.
ant: welcome

15. **facetious** (fə sē′ shəs) *adj.* comical; jocular; flippant
Her *facetious* comments were beginning to get tiresome.
syn: joking, witty, jocose *ant:* solemn, serious

Exercise I Words in Context

Fill in the blanks with the correct vocabulary words needed to complete the sentences.

enervated **endemic** **elixir** **empirical** **elucidated** **empathy**

A. The ________________ given to the boys to improve their ________________ condition that had been caused by the heat and humidity was an age-old secret. No one knew why it worked, and there was not any ________________ data to explain its miraculous benefits.

B. I feel great ________________ for women who are not getting equal pay for equal work. The problem is not ________________ to one company or industry; it is found in all areas of employment. The problem will remain with us until all of the issues have been ________________ and the view toward women in the workplace has been changed.

erotic **eschew** **emanate** **ennui**

C. The music seemed to ________________ from the dark woods. It had a soft, ________________ aura that turned his sense of ________________ to one of interest. He didn't know if he should mentally embrace or ________________ this strange, unreal, and somewhat frightening feeling.

epitome **emendations** **ephemeral** **facetious** **ergo**

D. Jim was the ________________ of the class clown. His ________________ remarks were a source of great annoyance to the teacher.

E. The editor made a number of ________________ in the text. He decided that this would not be one of those ________________ books that burns brightly for a short time and then disappears; ________________, he felt that the time he spent on it was well worth it.

Exercise II Roots, Prefixes, and Suffixes

Study the entries, and answer the questions that follow.

The root *equ* means "equal."
The root *fer* means "bear," "carry."
The root *flect/flex* means "bend."
The root *anim* means "mind."
The prefix *trans–* means "across."
The prefix *de–* means "away."
The prefix *dis–* means "apart, away."
The prefix *e–* means "out, up."
The prefix *re–* means "back."
The prefix *in–* means "in" or "not."

1. A person showing *equanimity* probably treats people with a ____________________; however, even he may lose an objective ____________________ if insulted.

2. List other words with *equ* as a root.

3. Literally, *transfer* means ____________________, while to ____________________ means "to carry back," and "to carry away from" (as in a reading passage) is to ____________________, but "to put it off" is to ____________________ it.

4. A person who cannot bend is said to be ____________________, but that which is bent or turned from a direct line is ____________________ or ____________________, and that which is bent back is ____________________. When one contracts a muscle, he is said to be ____________________ his muscles.

Exercise III Usage Inferences

Choose the answer that best suits the situation.

1. Which profession is a person most likely to show *empathy* for someone else?
   A. a retail clerk at Christmas
   B. a traffic policeman
   C. a nurse
   D. a judge

2. Which teenager in the situation described is probably demonstrating the greatest amount of *ennui*?
   A. Martha, who just won the state tennis championship
   B. Edith, who is watching the clock during French class
   C. Ruth, who just described how much she hates gym
   D. June, whose father has just bought her a car

Exercise IV Reading Comprehension

Read the selection and answer the questions.

The aristocracy Burke defended, in spite of the political marriages by which it tried to secure breeding for itself, had its mind undertrained by silly schoolmasters and governesses, its character corrupted by gratuitous luxury, its self respect adulterated to complete spuriousness by flattery and flunkeyism. It is no better today and never will be any better; our very peasants have something morally hardier in them that culminates occasionally in a Bunyan, a Burns, or a Carlyle. But observe this aristocracy, which was overpowered from 1832 to 1885 by the middle class, has come back to power by the votes of "the swinish multitude." Tom Paine has triumphed over Edmund Burke; and the swine are now courted electors. How many of their own class have these electors sent to parliament? Hardly a dozen out of 670, and these only under the persuasion of conspicuous personal qualifications and popular eloquence. The multitude thus pronounces judgment on its own units: it admits itself unfit to govern, and will vote only for a man morphologically and generically transfigured by palatial residence and equipage, by transcendent tailoring, by the glamour of aristocratic kinship. Well, we know these transfigured persons, these college passmen, these well groomed Algys and Bobbies, these cricketers to whom age brings golf instead of wisdom, these plutocratic products of "the nail and sarspan business as he got his money by." Do you know whether to laugh or cry at the notion that they, poor devils, will drive a team of continents as they drive a four-in-hand; turn a jostling anarchy of casual trade and speculation into an ordered productivity; and federate our colonies into a world-Power of the first magnitude? Give these people the most perfect political constitution and the soundest political program that benevolent omniscience can devise for them, and they will interpret it into mere fashionable folly or canting charity as infallibly as a savage converts the philosophical theology of a Scotch missionary into crude African idolatry.

–George Bernard Shaw

1. About the British aristocracy, the author feels
   A. great admiration.
   B. some sympathy.
   C. complete indifference.
   D. mild warmth.
   E. amused contempt.

2. The term "swinish multitude" refers to the
   A. criminal element.
   B. voters from the middle class.
   C. wealthy aristocrats.
   D. voters from the lower class.
   E. paid politicians and their supporters.

3. The author states or implies that
   A. Tom Paine and Edmund Burke were friends.
   B. the lower classes rarely elect one of their own to a position of power.
   C. Burns, Bunyan, and Carlyle were all from the lower class.
   D. even given the best of conditions, the present aristocratic establishment could not run the country effectively.
   E. B, C, and D are correct.

4. We can infer from this selection and the last that Shaw admires
   A. the aristocrats.
   B. the poor.
   C. Edward Burke.
   D. Tom Paine.
   E. Both A and B are correct.

Lesson Seven

1. **factious** (făk′ shəs) *adj.* causing disagreement
   We tried not to be *factious*, but we just couldn't agree with the speaker.

2. **fastidious** (fă stĭd′ ē əs) *adj.* hard to please; fussy
   My neighbor is a *fastidious* housekeeper.
   syn: meticulous, exacting *ant:* casual, lax

3. **fatuous** (făch′ ōō əs) *adj.* foolish, inane
   Her *fatuous* simperings began to grate on our nerves.
   syn: silly *ant:* sensible, wise

4. **fecund** (fē′ kənd) *adj.* fertile, productive
   The rabbits were very *fecund*, and we now have two dozen of them.
   syn: prolific *ant:* sterile

5. **ferret** (fĕr′ ĭt) *verb* to search or drive out
   noun a small animal of the weasel family
   Although Nate knew the answer was in the text, he just couldn't *ferret* it out.

6. **fervent** (fûr′ vənt) *adj.* eager, earnest
   We made a *fervent* attempt to capture the stallion, but he was too quick for us.
   syn: burning, passionate, ardent *ant:* apathetic

7. **fetish** (fĕt′ ĭsh) *noun* an object that receives respect or devotion
   The primitive tribes made a *fetish* of their totem poles.
   syn: charm, talisman

8. **finesse** (fĭ nĕs′) *noun* diplomacy; tact; artful management
   The diplomat was given the task because his superiors felt he had the necessary *finesse.*
   syn: skill, cunning *ant:* tactlessness

9. **fiscal** (fĭs′ kəl) *adj.* pertaining to finances
   This was the accountant's busiest time because it was the end of the company's *fiscal* year.

10. **fissure** (fĭsh′ ər) *noun* an opening; a groove; a split
    The small *fissure* in the tank was cause for great alarm.

11. **flaccid** (flă′ sĭd) *adj.* flabby
    The retired athlete now had *flaccid* muscles because he refused to work out.
    syn: weak, feeble *ant:* solid, taut

12. **flagellate** (flă′ jə lāt) *verb* to whip; lash
The boy's father never beat him, but would *flagellate* him verbally.
syn: flog

13. **flaunt** (flônt) *verb* to show off
Some people *flaunt* their wealth.
syn: boast, exhibit *ant:* conceal

14. **flout** (flout) *verb* to ridicule; show contempt for
He broke the rules and *flouted* all authority, and now he has to pay.
syn: mock, scoff *ant:* esteem, revere

15. **foment** (fō mĕnt′) *verb* to stir up; incite
At the convention, people were hired to *foment* disruptions during the senator's speech.
syn: instigate, arouse *ant:* quell, curb

Exercise I Words in Context

Fill in the blanks with the correct vocabulary words needed to complete the sentences.

factious **fastidious** **fetish** **finesse**

A. My mother is a ________________ housekeeper, but she makes a ________________ out of clean floors. I have tried to tell her that she doesn't need to wash and wax them so often, but I must lack ________________, because all I have been able to accomplish is to bring a ________________ element to our relationship.

flaunt **fatuous** **fervent** **fiscally**

B. I have a ________________ need to become ________________ responsible. My problem is that I like to ________________ what I have, so I buy things that are showy and expensive. I know this is ________________ on my part, but I can't seem to change.

flaccid **foment** **fissure** **flagellating** **fecund** **flout** **ferrets**

C. Daniel wanted to buy pair of ________________ but was concerned that they might be too ________________ and he would end up with more than he could handle.

D. When the governor accused the farm workers of trying to ________________ a riot, he caused a deep ________________ in his party between those who supported the striking farm workers and those who did not. Many people in his own party thought he was verbally ________________ the workers in order to get the support of the wealthy ranchers.

E. He used to ________________ all authority, and when they warned him about the dangers of taking steroids, he ignored them. Now he has ruined his health, and ________________ muscles are the least of his problems.

Exercise II Roots, Prefixes, and Suffixes

Study the entries and answer the questions that follow.

The root *fug* means "flee."
The root *grad/gress* means "step," "go."
The root *fus* means "pour."
The prefix *re–* means "again."
The prefix *in–* means "into."
The prefix *de–* means "out" or "away."
The prefix *e(x)–* means "out, away."

1. One who flees the law is a ____________________, while someone who has fled from a war is a ____________________.

2. The literal meaning of *fusion* is ____________________. If you are *effusive*, you ____________________; and if you pour something in or into, you ____________________ it; but if you pour (or take) it out, you ____________________ it.

3. List other words that contain *grad* and *gress*.

Exercise III Usage Inferences

Choose the answer that best suits the situation.

1. Which person is likely to be regarded as *fatuous*?
   A. a baker who bakes only pies and cakes
   B. a painter who is concerned only with making money
   C. someone who preaches that the earth is the center of the universe
   D. a comedian who specializes in doing comic impressions of famous people

2. Which is the best example of *finesse*?
   A. bank robbers who blow up a bank vault
   B. a barber who gives a good haircut
   C. a salesman who says just the right thing to make a sale
   D. a kite that rises into the sky

3. Which is the best example of a rule being *flouted*?
   A. Someone parks his car in front of a no-parking sign.
   B. After a long trial, a lawyer gives his closing arguments.
   C. Factory workers go on strike to protest low pay.
   D. A policeman gives a speeding ticket to someone going two miles over the limit.

Exercise IV Reading Comprehension

Read the selection and answer the questions.

The plot! A good plot is that sure edifice which slowly rises out of the interplay of circumstance on temperament, and temperament on circumstance, within the enclosing atmosphere of an idea. A human being is the best plot there is; it may be impossible to see why he is a good plot, because the idea within which he was brought forth cannot be fully grasped; but it is plain that he is a good plot. He is organic. And so it must be with a good play. Reason alone produces no good plots; they come by original sin, sure conception, and instinctive power. A bad plot, on the other hand, is simply a row of stakes, with a character impaled on each; characters who would have liked to live, but came to untimely grief; who started bravely, but fell on these stakes, placed beforehand in a row, and were transfixed one by one while their ghosts stride on, squeaking and gibbering, through the play. Whether these stakes are made of facts or of ideas, according to the nature of the dramatist who planted them, their effect on the unfortunate characters is the same; the creatures were begotten to be staked, and staked they are! The demand for a good plot, not infrequently heard, commonly signifies: "Tickle my sensations by stuffing the play with arbitrary adventures, so that I need not be troubled to take the characters seriously. Set the persons of the play to action, regardless of time, sequence, atmosphere, and probability!"

Now, true dramatic action is what characters do, at once contrary, as it were, to expectation, and yet because they have already done other things. No dramatist should let his audience know what is coming; but neither should he suffer his characters to act without making his audience feel that those are in harmony with temperament, and arise from previous known actions, together with the temperaments and previous known actions of the other characters in the play. The dramatist who hangs his characters to his plot, instead of hanging his plot to his characters, is guilty of cardinal sin.

The dialogue! Good dialogue again is character, marshaled so as continually to stimulate interest or excitement. The reason good dialogue is seldom found in plays is merely that it is hard to write, for it requires not only knowledge of what interests or excites, but such a feeling for character as brings misery to the dramatist's heart when his creations speak as they should not speak—ashes to his mouth when they say things for the sake of saying them—disgust when they are "smart."

–George Bernard Shaw

1. We may infer that for this author, the heart of any play is
   A. an action-filled plot.
   B. dialogue.
   C. characterization.
   D. style.
   E. theme.

2. The author states or implies that
   A. characters should grow naturally from the plot.
   B. the plot should develop naturally from the action of the characters.
   C. good dialogue sounds right in the characters' mouths.
   D. plots with action are preferable to those without action.
   E. Both B and C are correct.

3. The author uses the metaphor of the stakes to make the point that
   A. plot action must move forward quickly.
   B. characters cannot be used to mouth the ideas of the playwright.
   C. Both A and B are correct.
   D. a good play, like good meat or fish, must be served fresh.
   E. A, B, and D are correct.

4. The author states or implies that in a play, the dramatic action must
   A. let the audience know what is coming.
   B. be in harmony with the actions and temperament of the characters.
   C. be in harmony with the temperament and previous actions of the characters.
   D. Both B and C are correct.
   E. A, B, and C are correct.

Lesson Eight

1. **fop** (fŏp) *noun* an excessively fashion-conscious man
He was such a *fop* that he would wear only designer clothes.
syn: dandy

2. **fortuitous** (fôr tōō΄ ĭ təs) *adj.* lucky; by chance
My father said meeting my mother was *fortuitous*; my mother said it was fate.
syn: accidental, unexpected *ant:* premeditated, intentional

3. **gambol** (găm΄ bəl) *verb* to frolic; to romp about playfully
The pre-schoolers liked to *gambol* about on the playground.
syn: play, caper, rollick

4. **garish** (găr΄ ish) *adj.* tastelessly gaudy
The gypsy costumes were too *garish* for my taste.
syn: showy, glaring, flashy *ant:* sedate, conservative

5. **garner** (gär΄ nər) *verb* to gather, to acquire
During the fall harvest, it was the job of all the family to *garner* the crops.

6. **garrulous** (găr΄ ə ləs) *adj.* talkative
The little girl was so *garrulous* that we thought she would never stop talking.
syn: loquacious, verbose *ant:* taciturn

7. **germane** (jər mān΄) *adj.* relevant; fitting
Make sure that all of your answers are *germane* to the questions.
syn: appropriate, pertinent, suitable *ant:* irrelevant

8. **gibe** (jīb) *verb* to scoff, to ridicule
His favorite pastime was to *gibe* at everything his wife said.
syn: jeer, taunt, sneer *ant:* compliment, praise

9. **gloat** (glōt) *verb* to look at or think about with great satisfaction
The track team *gloated* over their latest victory.
syn: revel, crow *ant:* belittle

10. **glower** (glou΄ ər) *verb* to stare angrily
The boy *glowered* at his mother when she corrected his manners.
syn: frown, scowl *ant:* grin

11. **grandiose** (grăn′ dē ōs) *adj.* impressive, showy, magnificent
The young married couple wanted to buy the house, but their parents felt it was too *grandiose* for their lifestyle.

12. **gratuitous** (grə tōō′ ĭ təs) *adj.* unnecessary or uncalled for
He was always giving *gratuitous* advice whether someone wanted his opinion or not.

13. **grotesque** (grō tesk′) *adj.* absurd; distorted
The boy made a *grotesque* face behind the teacher's back.

14. **gumption** (gŭmp′ shən) *noun* courage and initiative; common sense
It takes a lot of *gumption* to succeed in this fast-paced society.
syn: enterprise, aggressiveness

15. **hackneyed** (hăk′ nēd) *adj.* commonplace; overused
"Good as gold" is a *hackneyed* expression.
syn: trite, banal *ant:* fresh, imaginative

Exercise I Words in Context

Fill in the blanks with the correct vocabulary words needed to complete the sentences.

gumption **germane** **glower** **gratuitous** **hackneyed** **gloating**

A. My father always gave ________________ advice to me. He was always going on about ________________ and initiative being important to success. He used a lot of ________________ expressions such as "do unto others," while I used to ________________ at him in my anger. I never felt that what he said to me was going to be ________________ to my life. How old-fashioned he was! Now, twenty years later, I hear myself saying to my son, "Neither a borrower nor a lender be," and I can see in my mind my father ________________.

garnering **grotesque** **garish** **gamboling** **garrulous**

B. One Halloween, Joanne dressed up in a very ________________ gypsy costume, convinced that she was the prettiest five-year-old in the world. She had always been ________________, so I knew that she would have no trouble ________________ her share of treats. Out she went, ________________ about with her friends while waiting for her mother to chaperone the group of pixies, ghosts, and the one little boy in his ________________ monster costume.

grandiose **fortuitous** **gibes** **foppish**

C. At the annual horse race, William's elaborate suit gave him a ________________ appearance, and Lauren wore a dress with gloves and a fancy hat. No one made ________________ about their old-fashioned and overly ________________ outfits because it was all part of the fun and tradition of the 100-year-old event. Tickets to the popular race were expensive, but the ________________ couple had won theirs in a contest.

Exercise II Roots, Prefixes, and Suffixes

Study the entries and answer the questions that follow.

The root *integr* means "entire" "whole."
The root *lat* means "carry."
The root *leg/lig/lect* means "choose," "gather."
The prefix *dis–* means "apart."
The prefix *trans–* means "across."

1. Something that is brought together as a whole is ________________, but if it is broken up or separated, it is ________________. A person who is morally whole is said to have ________________.

2. The literal meaning of *translation* is ________________. If one is carried upward in joy, he is said to be ________________; but if a message is to be carried back to someone, it is to be ________________.

3. One who is chosen is said to be ________________; and if one gathers items up, he is said to be ________________ them.

Exercise III Usage Inferences

Choose the answer that best suits the situation.

1. A *fop* would best describe a
   A. man wearing a hat with an ostrich feather.
   B. woman with a very expensive and rare fur coat.
   C. man wearing a tuxedo.
   D. woman in a sequined evening gown.

2. Which issue is the most *germane* when planning the interior renovation of a house?
   A. the town's climate
   B. the size of the lot
   C. the cost of a new house in the same area
   D. the cost of materials needed

3. Which is the best example of someone showing *gumption*?
   A. A runner wins his second race.
   B. A hunter calls his friends in government to protest new commercial developments.
   C. A person decides to pay a traffic ticket he did not deserve.
   D. A shy person speaks up in a meeting to defend a friend.

Exercise IV Reading Comprehension

Read the selection and answer the questions.

My scheme of *Order* gave me the most trouble. I found that, though it might be practicable where a man's business was such as to leave him the disposition of his time, that of a journeyman printer for instance, it was not possible to be followed by a person, who must mix with the world and often receive people of business at their own hours. *Order,* too, with regard to places for things, papers etc., I found extremely difficult to acquire. I had not been early accustomed to it, and, having an exceeding good memory, I was not so sensible of the inconvenience attending want of method. This article, therefore, cost me so much, and I made so little progress in amendment, and had such frequent relapses, that I was almost ready to give up the attempt, and content myself with a faulty character in that respect, like the man who, in buying an ax of a smith, my neighbor, desired to have the whole of its surface as bright as the edge. The smith consented to grind it bright for him if he would turn the wheel; he turned, while the smith pressed the broad face of the ax hard and heavily on the stone, which made the turning of it very fatiguing. The man came every now and then from the wheel to see how the work went on, and at length would take his ax as it was, without further grinding. "No," said the smith, "turn on, turn on; we shall have it bright by and by; as yet, it is only speckled." "Yes," says the man, "but I think I like a speckled ax best."

And I believe this may have been the case with many who, having, for want of some such means as I employed, found the difficulty of obtaining good and breaking bad habits in other points of vice and virtue, have given up the struggle, and concluded that *"a speckled ax was best"* for something, that pretended to be reason, was every now and then suggesting to me that such extreme nicety as I exacted for myself might be a kind of foppery in morals, which, if it were known would make me ridiculous; that a perfect character might be attended with the inconvenience of being envied and hated; and that a benevolent man should allow a few faults in himself, to keep his friends in countenance.

–Benjamin Franklin

1. In this selection, it is the author's intention to
   A. learn how to give and take orders.
   B. find a place for everything, and keep everything in its place.
   C. provide an order, an organization, for his life so that he is more efficient.
   D. Both A and B are correct.
   E. Both B and C are correct.

2. The speckled ax metaphor is used to illustrate the point that
   A. sometimes it is better to stop short of our goal because the energy required to reach the goal doesn't justify the added expenditure.
   B. while we may sharpen our own skills, we cannot expect others to be as diligent.
   C. while our neighbor may know his own business, we are the best judge of ours.
   D. a speckled ax can cut as sharply as a bright one as long as the axman knows what he is doing.
   E. sometimes we have to look closely, but there is beauty in everything, and it is there for those who look.

3. The last paragraph in this selection could be a good example of
   A. an allegory.
   B. an epic.
   C. a rationalization.
   D. a hyperbolic statement.
   E. a non sequitur.

4. The author states or implies that
   A. no one truly knows another.
   B. a perfect person would be disliked by his friends.
   C. people are people on the inside where it counts.
   D. two wrongs only produce another wrong.
   E. Both A and C are correct.

Lesson Nine

1. **halcyon** (hăl′ sē ən) *adj.* calm, pleasant
   The *halcyon* days of last month contrasted with the turbulent days of this month.
   syn: tranquil, unruffled *ant:* troubled, tumultuous

2. **hallow** (hăl′ ō) *verb* to make holy
   adj. holy
   We cannot *hallow* this field, for the men who died here made it holy.
   Many colleges refer to their buildings as *hallowed* halls of learning.
   syn: bless, consecrate *ant:* desecrate

3. **harbinger** (här′ bĭn jər) *noun* an omen or sign
   The presence of the black cat was taken as a *harbinger* of bad luck.
   syn: portent

4. **harlequin** (här′ lə kən) *noun* a clown
   One of Picasso's famous paintings, *Harlequin*, is a painting of an old-fashioned clown.

5. **hector** (hĕk′ tər) *verb* to bully; pester
   Unless you stand up to him, that bully will *hector* you the entire year.
   syn: browbeat

6. **hedonism** (hēd′ n ĭz əm) *noun* the pursuit of pleasure, especially of the senses
   John believed in *hedonism*, rather than self-sacrifice.

7. **hegira** (hĭ jī′ rə) *noun* flight, escape
   During the Vietnam War, there was a *hegira* to Canada by people opposed to the war.

8. **hermetic** (hər mĕt′ ĭk) *adj.* tightly sealed
   That medicine should be packed in *hermetic* containers.
   syn: airtight

9. **heterogeneous** (hĕt ər ə jē′ nē əs) *adj.* different; dissimilar
   The squad of soldiers in a typical war movie is a *heterogeneous* group of young men from quite varied backgrounds.
   syn: diverse, varied *ant:* homogeneous, similar

10. **hiatus** (hī ā′ təs) *noun* a pause or gap
    During the summer *hiatus*, the cast of the television show was free to pursue other interests.

11. **hoi polloi** (hoi pə loi′) *noun* common people; the masses
    The *hoi polloi* in Rome loved to watch the Christians fight the lions.

12. **hospice** (hŏs′ pĭs) *noun* a place or a program for the terminally ill; a shelter
The new *hospice* for cancer patients opened in July.

13. **hubris** (hyōō′ brĭs) *noun* excessive pride or self-confidence
The Greek warriors were known for their *hubris* and their fierceness in battle.
syn: haughtiness, arrogance *ant:* humility, diffidence

14. **hybrid** (hī′ brĭd) *noun* anything of mixed origin
adj. mixed, assorted
The prize-winning roses were *hybrids*, combining the best whites and reds.
The *hybrid* cars could run on gasoline or electricity.

15. **idiosyncrasy** (ĭ dē ə sĭn′ krə sē) *noun* a peculiar personality trait
Hiding money in tin cans was only one of the old man's *idiosyncrasies*.

Exercise I Words in Context

Fill in the blanks with the correct vocabulary words needed to complete the sentences.

hegira **hermetically** **halcyon** **hedonism** **harbinger**

A. The cool weather of the first days of September marked the end of the ________________ days of summer and was an unwelcome ________________ of fall. Leaving the ________________ of their vacations behind, people reversed the ________________ to the beaches and returned home to resume life in their ________________ sealed offices in the city.

hubris **idiosyncratic** **hybrids** **heterogeneous**

B. In his greenhouse, he grew ________________, of which he was justly proud. Unfortunately, the neighborhood parties were made up of a(n) ________________ group of people, some of whom knew little or nothing about flowers. They interpreted his pride as arrogance and said that he was filled with ________________. And, although his wife had warned him that his behavior made him appear ________________, he paid little attention to her comments.

hiatus **hectoring** **hallowed** **harlequins** **hoi polli** **hospice**

C. The _________________ was opened for all who needed shelter during that cold spell last winter. The founder of the group running the shelter was on _________________ from his job as an accountant. When the shelter first opened, the neighborhood _________________ came out in full force, _________________ the employees and clients because the residents did not want this shelter in their neighborhood.

D. The famous entertainment troupe, with its spectacular acrobats and colorful _________________, performed its final show of the year at the most _________________ theater in the city.

Exercise II Roots, Prefixes, and Suffixes

Study the entries and answer the questions that follow.

The root *merge* means "plunge," "sink."
The root *migr* means "wander."
The root *mir* means "look."
The root *mon* means "advise," "remind."
The prefix *sub–* means "under."
The prefix *ad–* means "towards."
The prefix *re–* means "again."
The prefix *e–* means "out of."

1. Literally, a *monitor* is _____________________; and if you *admonish* someone, you _____________________

2. List three words that contain the root *migr.*

3. Give the literal meaning of the following:
   reemergence
   submerge
   merge
   emerge
   mergence
   admiration

Exercise III Usage Inferences

Choose the answer that best suits the situation.

1. Which place is most likely to be described as *hallowed*?
   A. a civil war battlefield
   B. an isolated mountain top
   C. a historic train station
   D. a creepy old house

2. Who is most likely to be the victim of a *hectoring* mob?
   A. a politician at a state fair
   B. a judge during a controversial trial
   C. police officers on the scene of an accident
   D. an umpire who makes a bad decision

3. Which behavior is most likely to be described as an *idiosyncrasy*?
   A. getting to work on time every day
   B. always counting to five before touching a doorknob
   C. reading a chapter of a book before going to sleep
   D. preferring chicken to beef

Exercise IV Reading Comprehension

Read the selection and answer the questions.

Culture is activity of thought, and receptiveness to beauty and humane feeling. Scraps of information have nothing to do with it. A merely well-informed man is the most useless bore on God's earth. What we should aim at producing is men who possess both culture and expert knowledge in some special direction. Their expert knowledge will give them the ground to start from, and their culture will lead them as deep as philosophy and as high as art. We have to remember that the valuable intellectual development is self-development, and that it mostly takes place between the ages of sixteen and thirty. As to training, the most important part is given by mothers before the age of twelve. A saying of Archbishop Temple illustrates my meaning. Someone expressed surprise at the success of a man, who as a boy at Rugby had been somewhat undistinguished. He answered, "It is not what they are at eighteen, it is what they become afterwards that matters."

In training a child to activity of thought, above all things we must beware of what I will call "inert ideas" — that is to say, ideas that are merely received into the mind without being utilized, or tested, or thrown into fresh combinations.

In the history of education, the most striking phenomenon is that schools of learning, which at one epoch are alive with a ferment of genius, in a succeeding generation exhibit merely pedantry and routine. The reason is, that they are overladen with inert ideas. Education with inert ideas is not only useless: it is, above all things harmful — *Corruptio optimi, pessima.* Except at rare intervals of intellectual ferment, education in the past has been radically infected with inert ideas. That is the reason why uneducated clever women, who have seen much of the world, are in middle life the most cultured part of the community. They have been saved from this horrible burden of inert ideas. Every intellectual revolution which has ever stirred humanity into greatness has been a passionate protest against inert ideas. Then, alas, with pathetic ignorance of human psychology, it has proceeded by some educational scheme to bind humanity afresh with inert ideas of its own fashioning.

Let us now ask how in our system of education we are to guard against this mental dryrot. We enunciate two educational commandments, "Do not teach too many subjects," and again, "What you teach, teach thoroughly."

–Alfred North Whitehead

1. The main point in this selection is that
   A. education must avoid "inert ideas."
   B. one of the major aims of education is the development of intellectual thought in the student.
   C. there are two ways to avoid the teaching of inert ideas.
   D. schools that once were good are now loaded down with inert ideas.
   E. in the training of the young, we must look to the history of education.

2. The tone of this selection may be best described as one of
   A. angry denunciation.
   B. sad resignation.
   C. passionate protest.
   D. calm reflection.
   E. patient understanding.

3. The author states or implies that
   A. the great revolutions have been a protest against inert ideas.
   B. uneducated, clever women are better off not having had an education in inert ideas.
   C. anything that is taught, ought to be taught thoroughly.
   D. Both B and C are correct.
   E. A, B, and C are correct.

4. To combat inert ideas, schools must
   A. not teach too many subjects.
   B. teach thoroughly that which they teach.
   C. Both A and B are correct.
   D. always strive to bring in new people.
   E. constantly question their goals.

VOCABULARY for the College Bound

Lesson Ten

1. **idolatry** (ī dol´ ə trē) *noun* excessive or blind adoration; the worship of an object
When the people began to worship the statue, the priest accused them of *idolatry*.

2. **ignoble** (ĭg nō´ bəl) *adj.* dishonorable, shameful
Cheating on an exam is an *ignoble* way to get good grades.
syn: despicable, base *ant:* noble, glorious

3. **imminent** (ĭm´ ə nənt) *adj.* likely to happen; threatening
Although danger was *imminent*, the crew seemed quite relaxed.
syn: impending, close *ant:* distant, delayed

4. **immolate** (ĭm´ ə lāt) *verb* to kill as a sacrifice, often by fire
Some Buddhist monks *immolated* themselves as their form of protest against the government's policies.

5. **immutable** (ĭ myōō´ tə bəl) *adj.* unchangeable, fixed
The laws of nature are *immutable.*
syn: enduring *ant:* flexible, changeable

6. **impair** (ĭm pâr´) *verb* to weaken; to cause to become worse
Mothers used to say that reading in poor light could *impair* your vision.
syn: damage; deteriorate *ant:* enhance

7. **impale** (ĭm pāl´) *verb* to pierce through with a sharp, pointed object
With a sharp stick, the boy was able to *impale* a fish in the stream.

8. **impalpable** (ĭm păl´ pə bəl) *adj.* unable to be felt
The difference between the two sound systems is *impalpable* to most people.
syn: intangible

9. **impecunious** (ĭm pĭ kyōō´ nē əs) *adj.* without money; penniless
Although *impecunious*, his pride kept him from asking for help.
syn: destitute, indigent *ant:* affluent, prosperous

10. **impediment** (ĭm pĕd´ ə mənt) *noun* a barrier; an obstruction
The supervisor wouldn't be an *impediment* to her advancement.
syn: obstacle, hindrance *ant:* aid

11. **imperative** (ĭm pĕr´ ə tĭv) *adj.* extremely necessary; vitally important
It is *imperative* that you leave immediately.

12. **imperious** (ĭm pîr′ ē əs) *adj.* domineering; haughty
The judge pronounced his findings in an *imperious* voice.
syn: overbearing, arrogant, masterful *ant:* servile, submissive

13. **impinge** (ĭm pĭnj′) *verb* to strike; encroach
The new leash law was viewed by Mr. Jackson as *impinging* on his constitutional rights.

14. **impious** (ĭm′ pē əs) *adj.* disrespectful toward God
He considered laughing in church *impious* behavior.
syn: irreligious, profane *ant:* devout, pious

15. **importune** (ĭm pôr to͞on′) *verb* to persistently ask; beg
John *importuned* his father, but could not get the car keys.

Exercise I Words in Context

Fill in the blanks with the correct vocabulary words needed to complete the sentences.

immutable **impale** **impecunious** **impious** **imminent** **importune** **imperiously**

A. The storm, judging from the darkness in the sky, was ________________. The lightning seemed to ________________ the earth with its ferocity. The old barn, however, stood ________________ at the end of the field as though daring the ________________ laws of nature to do their worst.

B. Although the man was ________________, one could not tell that by his manner or dress. It would never occur to him, even at his worst moments, to ________________ God for intercession. He would have felt such a request to be an ________________ act.

impalpable	**impediment**	**ignoble**	**immolate**
impinge	**imperative**	**idolatry**	**impaired**

C. As I entered the room, I heard my father say "Yes, ________________ often leads to strange excesses. One tribe I spent some time with would go out and kidnap one of their enemies. Then, in the light of a full moon, they would tie the poor victim to a stake and ________________ him. Not frequently," he concluded, "rationality is ________________ by religious ardor."

D. "Sometimes," the guru was saying, "there is something in the air that is ________________ to ordinary mortals, but easily felt by the trained believer."
"Nonsense," I said. "That kind of talk is a major ________________ to clear thinking."

E. I said, "It is ________________ that we find the key. If we cannot find it, I will be forced to ________________ on the kindness of our neighbors."
"Could you be so ________________," Jack replied, "as to go and beg something from people that you know despise you, and whom you despise?"

Exercise II Roots, Prefixes, and Suffixes

Study the entries and answer the questions that follow.

The root *mut* means "change."
The root *pel* means "drive."
The root *oper* means "work."
The root *pet* means "seek."
The prefix *in/im–* can mean "against" or "not."
The prefix *pro–* means "forward."
The prefix *con/com–* means "with."
The prefix *dis–* means "away."
The prefix *trans–* means "across."
The prefix *re–* means "back."

1. A *mutation* is ____________________; if you change one thing to another, you have engaged in ____________________; but if something (a law of nature, for example) cannot be changed, it is said to be ____________________.

2. List words that contain the root *oper.*

3. If you drive something forward, you ____________________ it; but if you drive someone or something back, you are said to ____________________ it; and if you drive it away (an old wives' tale, for example), you ____________________ it. If you are driven to do something by something within you, you are ____________________; but if someone else forces you, then you are ____________________.

Exercise III Usage Inferences

Choose the answer that best suits the situation.

1. Which is the best example of something that is *imminent*?
   A. You have a doctor's appointment set for next Wednesday.
   B. You feel guilty for having forgotten your homework.
   C. You feel as if you are going to sneeze.
   D. You have to finish dinner before watching TV.

2. Which of the following is best described as *immutable*?
   A. the speed that light travels
   B. the cost of mailing a letter
   C. the height of a child
   D. the speed limit on interstate highways

Exercise IV Reading Comprehension

Read the selection and answer the questions.

Still we live meanly, like ants. Our life is frittered away by detail. An honest man has hardly need to count more than his ten fingers, or in extreme cases he may add his ten toes, and lump the rest. Simplicity, simplicity, simplicity! I say, let your affairs be as two or three, and not a hundred or a thousand; instead of a million count half a dozen, and keep your accounts on your thumbnail. In the midst of this chopping sea of civilized life, such are the clouds and storms and quicksands and thousand-and-one items to be allowed for; a man, if he would not flounder and go to the bottom must be a great calculator indeed who succeeds. Simplify, simplify. Instead of three meals a day, if it be necessary eat but one; instead of a hundred dishes, five; and reduce other things in proportion. Our life is like a German Confederacy, made up of petty states, with its boundary forever fluctuating, so that even a German cannot tell you how it is bounded at any moment. The nation itself, with all its so-called internal improvements, which by the way, are all external and superficial, is just such an unwieldy and overgrown establishment, cluttered with furniture and tripped up by its own traps, ruined by luxury and heedless expense, by want of calculation and a worthy aim, as the million households in the land; and the only cure for it as for them is in a rigid economy, a stern and more than Spartan simplicity of life and elevation of purpose. It lives too fast. Men think that it is essential that the Nation have commerce, and export ice, and talk through a telegraph, and ride thirty miles an hour, without a doubt, whether they do or not; but whether we should live like baboons or like men, is a little uncertain. If we do not get out sleepers, and forge rails, and devote days and nights to the work, but go to tinkering upon our lives to improve them, who will build railroads? And if railroads are not built, how shall we get to heaven in season? But if we stay at home and mind our business, who will want railroads? We do not ride on the railroad; it rides upon us...

–Henry David Thoreau

1. In this selection, the author compares civilized life to
   A. that of ants.
   B. a chopping sea.
   C. Both A and B are correct.
   D. the German Confederacy.
   E. All of the above are correct.

2. The author' s main point in this selection is that he believes
   A. work is not only necessary, but also ennobling.
   B. that we spend our lives working to acquire things, and it is this that propels the economy.
   C. we complicate our lives and waste our time on insignificant objects and activities.
   D. the nation is growing too large, too fast.
   E. most men think that it is essential that the nation have commerce.

3. The author states or implies that
   A. man would be better off devoting himself to improving his life than devoting himself to work.
   B. a simple life would be unencumbered by material things and the need to work to get more material things.
   C. Both A and B are correct.
   D. what most men see as progress (railroads, telegraphs, etc.) may not really represent progress to the thinking man.
   E. All of the above are correct.

4. In the last line in the selection, the author is suggesting that
   A. that which appears to be one thing, may actually be something quite different.
   B. whoever owns the railroad owns us.
   C. while progress for its own sake is a waste, progress for the sake of mankind is noble.
   D. when we devote our lives working to acquire things, the things do not belong to us; we belong to the things.
   E. All of the above are correct.

Lesson Eleven

1. **impotent** (ĭm′ pə tənt) *adj.* powerless; lacking strength
Without the gun, he felt *impotent.*
syn: ineffective, helpless *ant:* potent, powerful

2. **imprecation** (ĭm prĭ kā′ shən) *noun* a curse
Jennifer was so angry that she pronounced an *imprecation* on him, his family, and all his friends.

3. **jocular** (jŏk′ yə lər) *adj.* humorous, lighthearted
Dad was in such a good mood that we all enjoyed dinner because of his *jocular* manner.
syn: joking, witty, amusing *ant:* solemn, morose

4. **juxtapose** (jŭk′ stə pōz) *verb* to place side by side for comparison
People often *juxtapose* the pros and cons of something to help them make a decision.

5. **kinetic** (kĭ nĕt′ ĭk) *adj.* pertaining to motion
To demonstrate *kinetic* energy, he pushed a steel ball off the table.

6. **kismet** (kĭz′ mĕt) *noun* destiny; fate; fortune (one's lot in life)
He said that it was a lucky accident that they had met; she said it was *kismet.*

7. **knell** (nĕl) *noun* the sound of a bell rung slowly to indicate mourning or an end
Standing at the side of the grave in the rain, they could faintly hear the *knell* of a church bell.

8. **labyrinth** (lăb′ ə rĭnth) *noun* a complicated network of winding passages; a maze
The mice were made to run through a *labyrinth* in order to reach their food.

9. **lachrymose** (lăk′ rə mōs) *adj.* tearful, weepy
It was time for the girl to get over her *lachrymose* behavior and start smiling again.

10. **laconic** (lă kŏn′ ĭk) *adj.* using few words; short; concise
He was a *laconic* man who wasted few words.
syn: pithy, taciturn *ant:* verbose, loquacious

11. **lambent** (lăm′ bənt) *adj.* softly bright or radiant; running or moving lightly over a surface
Lambent flames gently enveloped the logs.

12. **languid** (lăng′ wĭd) *adj.* sluggish; drooping from weakness
The hot summer day made everyone feel *languid.*
syn: listless, feeble, drooping *ant:* robust, vigorous

13. **lascivious** (lă sĭv′ ē əs) *adj.* lustful or lewd; inciting sexual desire
The *lascivious* qualities of one district in the town made it an area that most people avoided.
syn: wanton, obscene *ant:* wholesome, decent

14. **legerdemain** (lej′ ər dĭ mān) *noun* sleight of hand; deception
The magician's act was an extraordinary feat of *legerdemain.*

15. **libertine** (lĭb′ ər tēn) *noun* one who leads an immoral life
During the day he pretended to be righteous, but at night he was a *libertine.*

Exercise I Words in Context

Fill in the blanks with the correct vocabulary words needed to complete the sentences.

jocular **imprecation** **laconic** **labyrinth** **impotent**

A. The police felt ________________ to do anything about the street crime in the neighborhood. It was as though a(n) ________________ had been cast on the entire ________________ of burned-out tenements and deserted storefronts.

B. The ________________ attitude of the teacher made all of the students feel good that day. Usually he was a(n) ________________ teacher who said what he had to say with the fewest possible words.

knell **lambent** **kinetic** **kismet** **languid**

C. The sun cast ________________ gleams on the water. It was a hot, humid day that made the throng of bathers ________________. But then, amidst this calm, one young one man suddenly jumped up and ran from blanket to blanket. It was as if he had suddenly been struck by some ________________ force that impelled him into action.

D. Ned heard the ________________ of the church bell as he was reading and thought it was ________________ that it had happened just as he reached the part where the main character died.

juxtaposed **lachrymose** **libertine** **legerdemain** **lascivious**

E. As I remembered her, she had been a ________________ child whose eyes were always red and swollen. Therefore, I was quite surprised when this beautiful young woman entered the room and said that she was Laura. At her side was a suave, continental man with a ________________ look in his eyes. I later learned that he was a ________________ who had squandered one fortune already and was quickly going through a second.

F. I must admit that the news article treated the controversial issue fairly. It presented the main points of one side, and then it ________________ the main points of the other side. Of course, the lunatic fringe had its usual complaint. They accused the newspaper of bias. But they see conspirators behind every bush and ________________ in any simple, straightforward action.

Exercise II Roots, Prefixes, and Suffixes

Study the entries and answer the questions that follow.

The root *petr* means "stone."
The root *pon/pos* means "place," "put."
The root *plic* means "fold," "bend."
The root *prehend/prehens* means "take," "grasp."
The root *glyph* means "writing."
The prefix *ex–* means "out."
The prefix *com–* means "together."
The prefix *in/im–* means "into."
The suffix *–fy* means "make."

1. Someone or something turned to stone is ____________________, so *petrifaction* is ____________________. If you were looking for a *petroglyph*, a good place to look would be ____________________; and *petrology* is ____________________.

2. Literally, something that is *complicated* is ____________________; and if you *implicate* someone, you have to ____________________; but if you wish to fold out (a passage in a book, for example), you are said to have ____________________ the passage.

3. List words that contain the root *pon/pos*.

4. Something that is *prehensile* is adapted for ____________________. List other words that contain the root *prehend/prehens*.

Exercise III Usage Inferences

Choose the answer that best suits the situation.

1. What is most likely to be called *jocular*?
   A. an expensive, but delicious, dinner
   B. a resort hotel featuring a famous actor
   C. a comedian on tour
   D. a trip to the grocery store

2. Which is probably the most *languid*?
   A. the best basketball player
   B. a fishing boat
   C. the editor of the town newspaper
   D. a hot, summer day

3. Which of the following is the best demonstration of *kinetic* energy?
   A. A wrecking ball destroys a building.
   B. A microwave oven cooks a frozen dinner.
   C. A balloon sticks to a sweater.
   D. A broken spring sits inside a watch.

Exercise IV Reading Comprehension

Read the selection and answer the questions.

I left the woods for as good a reason as I went there. Perhaps it seemed to me that I had several more lives to live, and could not spare any more time for that one. It is remarkable how easily and insensibly we fall into a particular route, and make a beaten track for ourselves. I had not lived there a week before my feet wore a path from my door to the pond side; and though it is five or six years since I trod it, it is still quite distinct. It is true, I fear that others may have fallen into it, and so helped to keep it open. The surface of the earth is soft and impressible by the feet of men; and so with the paths which the mind travels. How worn and dusty, then, must be the highways of the world, how deep the ruts of tradition and conformity! I did not wish to take a cabin passage, but rather to go before the mast and on the deck of the world, for there I could best see the moonlight amid the mountains. I do not wish to go below now.

I learned this, at least, by my experiment; that if one advances confidently in the direction of his dreams, and endeavors to live the life which he has imagined, he will meet with success unexpected in common hours. He will put some things behind, will pass an invisible boundary; new, universal, and more liberal laws will begin to establish themselves around and within him; or the old laws be expanded, and interpreted in his favor in a more liberal sense, and he will live with the license of a higher order of beings. In proportion as he simplifies his life, the laws of the universe will appear less complex, and solitude will not be solitude, nor poverty poverty, nor weakness weakness. If you have built castles in the air, your work need not be lost; that is where they should be. Now put the foundations under them...

–Henry David Thoreau

1. The author's main point is that
   A. dreaming can make our wishes truth.
   B. the route to a full life may sometimes be difficult, worn, and dusty.
   C. life is meant to be explored, not lived in a dull routine.
   D. Both B and C are correct.
   E. A, B, and C are correct.

2. In this selection, the author uses as a metaphor for life, living, and thinking
   A. tracks or paths.
   B. building castles.
   C. Both A and B are correct.
   D. a ship voyage.
   E. All of the above are correct.

3. The author states or implies that
   A. going into the woods to live was a mistake.
   B. one must follow his own inclinations or dreams.
   C. he left his house in the woods with many regrets.
   D. the more one simplifies his life, the less complex it becomes.
   E. Both B and D are correct.

4. The phrase "the ruts of tradition and conformity" refers to
   A. how his neighbors live.
   B. how he used to live.
   C. how he lives now.
   D. how most people think.
   E. Both B and C are correct.

BOOK C

VOCABULARY
for the College Bound

Lesson Twelve

1. **machination** (măk ə nā′ shən) *noun* an evil design or plan
Batman and Robin tried hard to figure out what new *machinations* the Joker had up his sleeve.
syn: scheme, plot, intrigue

2. **macroscopic** (măk rə skŏp′ ĭk) *adj.* visible to the naked eye
On a clear night, the Milky Way is *macroscopic*.
ant: microscopic

3. **maelstrom** (măl′ strəm) *noun* a whirlpool; turbulence
His emotions were like a *maelstrom*, and he couldn't decide what course to follow.

4. **malapropism** (măl′ ə prŏp ĭz əm) *noun* a word humorously misused
Her *malapropism* of describing him as very "effluent" instead of "affluent" amused everyone at the party.

5. **malleable** (măl′ ē ə bəl) *adj.* capable of being changed; easily shaped
The sculptor wanted to keep the clay *malleable* until the final design took form in his head.
syn: workable *ant:* rigid, inflexible

6. **martinet** (märt ə nĕt′) *noun* a strict disciplinarian; taskmaster
The teacher was a *martinet* who never made any exceptions to the rules.

7. **masochist** (măs′ ə kĭst) *noun* one who enjoys his or her own pain and suffering
Sue accused her friend of being a *masochist* because he refused to go to the doctor even though he had been sick for two weeks.

8. **mendacious** (mĕn dā′ shəs) *adj.* lying; false, deceitful
Everyone knew the politician was *mendacious*, yet the voters kept re-electing him.
syn: duplicitous *ant:* honest, truthful

9. **meretricious** (mĕr ĭ trĭsh′ əs) *adj.* attractive in a cheap, flashy way; false
The theory is tempting to believe, but I think it is *meretricious*.
syn: gaudy, showy, tawdry *ant:* restrained, tasteful

10. **milieu** (mēl′ yōō) *noun* environment, setting
The poet felt he was in his correct *milieu* as soon as he set foot in Paris.

11. **miscreant** (mĭs′ krē ənt) *noun* a vicious person
The police were looking for the *miscreant* in all of the local hangouts.
syn: villain, criminal, knave

12. **nebulous** (nĕb′ yə ləs) *adj.* hazy, vague, uncertain
He had a *nebulous* feeling of fear all day, but he didn't understand why until the thunder started.
syn: cloudy, indistinct, obscure *ant:* distinct, precise

13. **necromancy** (nĕk′ rə măn′ sē) *noun* magic, especially that practiced by a witch
The grieving son hoped to talk with his dead mother through the woman who practiced *necromancy.*
syn: black magic, conjuring

14. **neologism** (nē äl ə jĭz′əm) *noun* the creation or use of a new word or definition
Some writers coin *neologisms* to confuse and impress their readers.

15. **nihilism** (nī′ ə lĭz əm) *noun* a total rejection of established laws
Nihilism rejects established laws and order, but it offers nothing in their place.

Exercise I Words in Context

Fill in the blanks with the correct vocabulary words needed to complete the sentences.

malleable **nebulous** **martinet** **maelstrom** **machinations**

A. Hitler was known as a ________________ whose followers feared him. His ________________ for the control of Europe caused a ________________ throughout the world.

B. Some people believe that children are best taught at a very early age when they are still ________________. Others disagree. I believe the issue is quite ________________ and plan to research it further.

milieu **mendacious** **miscreants** **malapropisms** **masochist** **meretricious**

C. Although her conversation is filled with ________________, she is a kind and gentle soul. Her sister, however, is so ________________ that you cannot believe a word from her mouth.

D. "Oh, I will grant that your argument has a flashy attractiveness to it; but like a cheap steak that is all sizzle and little substance, it is ________________. A ________________," I continued, "is a sick person who needs help, not someone to be exploited."

E. Tom relaxed as he entered the room. The police station was his ________________, and he felt more comfortable questioning the ________________ he dealt with there than on their own turf.

nihilism **necromancy** **neologisms** **macroscopic**

F. As he looked at his arm, something bit him again; but he could see nothing. Then he saw it. It was a bug so tiny that it was barely ________________. He sighed with relief, for Sheila had convinced him that he was the victim of voodoo or some other form of ________________.

G. Carl always had to have some "ism" to believe in—fascism, then socialism, and now ________________. He was a charismatic man with little formal education. Although forceful when he spoke, Carl's lack of education was apparent. He used ________________ that impressed the ignorant but confused or annoyed more knowledgeable people. Carl coined words like "neosensate" and "narcoattributiveness" that had no real meaning to anyone but him.

Exercise II Roots, Prefixes, and Suffixes

Study the entries and answer the questions that follow.

The root *sent/sens* means "feel," "think."
The root *sequ/secut* means "follow."
The root *sist* means "place," "stand."
The prefix *proto–* means "before."

1. Literally, a *prototype* is a ____________________, and a *protagonist* in a story is a ____________________.

2. Someone who feels a great deal for or thinks of others is said to be ____________________, while a *sentient* person is ____________________. The word *intellectual* refers to the mind, while the word that refers to feelings or pleasures of the body (food or music, for example) is ____________________.

3. Literally, a *sequel* is ____________________.

4. List words that contain the root *sist*.

Exercise III Usage Inferences

Choose the answer that best suits the situation.

1. What activity is most likely to be described as a *machination*?
   A. A football coach teaches blocking skills.
   B. A newspaper editor puts a new reporter on a story.
   C. People trade places in line to be on the same team.
   D. Three boys build a rocket for class.

2. Who is more likely to come up with a *neologism*?
   A. a writer
   B. a soccer player
   C. a nuclear scientist
   D. a trumpet player

3. Which is most likely to be compared to a *maelstrom*?
   A. a long period of storms after a clear, warm summer night
   B. blowing the candles out on a cake
   C. a controversy surrounding illegal steroids
   D. a person who does an efficient job, but gets no recognition

4. Which of the following material is probably being used because it is *malleable*?
   A. silicone for solar panels
   B. oak for the mast of a sailing ship
   C. water for cooling an engine
   D. putty for filling cracks in walls

Exercise IV Reading Comprehension

Read the selection and answer the questions.

The human species, according to the best theory I can form of it, is composed of two distinct races, *the men who borrow*, and *the men who lend*. To these two original diversities may be reduced all those impertinent classifications of Gothic and Celtic tribes, white men, black men, red men. All the dwellers upon earth…naturally fall in with one or other of these primary distinctions. The infinite superiority of the former, which I choose to designate as the *great race*, is discernible in their figure…The latter are born degraded. "He shall serve his brethren." There is something in the air of one of this cast, lean and suspicious; contrasting with the open, trusting, generous manners of the other….

What a careless, even deportment hath your borrower!….What contempt for money, — accounting it (yours and mine especially) no better than dross! What a liberal confounding of those pedantic distinctions of *meum* and *tuum*! or rather what a noble simplification of language… resolving these supposed opposites into one clear, intelligible pronoun adjective!….

He is the true taxer who "calleth all the world up to be taxed:" and the distance is as vast between him and *one of us*, as subsisted betwixt the Augustan Majesty and the poorest [peasant]…His exactions, too, have such a cheerful, voluntary air! So far removed from your sour parochial or state-gatherers,—those ink-horn varlets, who carry their want of welcome in their faces! He cometh to you with a smile, and troubleth you with no receipt; confining himself to no set season….He applieth the *lene tormentum* of a pleasant look to your purse,—which to that gentle warmth expands her silken leaves, as naturally as the cloak of the traveller, for which sun and wind contended! He is the true Propontic which never ebbeth!…In vain the victim, whom he delighteth to honour, struggles with destiny; he is in the net. Lend therefore cheerfully, O man ordained to lend….When thou seest the proper authority coming, meet it smilingly, as it were half-way. Come, a handsome sacrifice! See how light he makes of it! Strain not courtesies with a noble enemy.

–Charles Lamb

1. In the first paragraph, when the author uses the term "former," he is referring to
   A. men who borrow money.
   B. men who lend money.
   C. Goths.
   D. Celts.
   E. Parthians.

2. The reader may infer that the *meum* and *tuum* (mine and yours) are resolved to the adjective
   A. his.
   B. her.
   C. my.
   D. theirs.
   E. ours.

3. The tone of this selection may be best described as one of
   A. angry impatience.
   B. righteous indignation.
   C. bitter resignation.
   D. biting sarcasm.
   E. gentle humor.

4. The term “ink-horn varlets” refers to
   A. borrowers.
   B. lenders.
   C. tax collectors.
   D. authors.
   E. none of the above.

VOCABULARY for the College Bound

Lesson Thirteen

1. **nirvana** (nûr vä′ nə) *noun* a condition of great peace or happiness
George was seeking *nirvana* to heal his wounded soul.

2. **nonentity** (nŏn ĕn′ tĭ tē) *noun* a person or thing of little importance
"I do exist," she yelled. "You treat me as a *nonentity*."

3. **non sequitur** (nŏn sĕk′ wĭ tər) *noun* something that does not logically follow
"That," said John, "is a *non sequitur*. Because he can't control his own family, it doesn't follow that he would make a poor mayor."

4. **nubile** (nōō′ bīl) *adj.* (regarding females) suitable for marriage in reference to age and development; young and attractive
In the last six years, she had grown from a short, thin twelve-year-old to a *nubile* young woman.

5. **obdurate** (ŏb′ də rət) *adj.* stubborn; hardhearted
The young boy was *obdurate* in his refusal to make any trade.
syn: inflexible, obstinate *ant:* compliant, amenable

6. **obfuscate** (ŏb′ fŭs kāt) *verb* to make unclear
The realtor tried to *obfuscate* the issue, and the confused buyer did not know if the seller had accepted his offer or not.
syn: muddle, obscure *ant:* clarify, elucidate

7. **obloquy** (ŏb′ lə kwē) *noun* strong disapproval; a bad reputation resulting from public criticism
His behavior brought shame to his family and *obloquy* on himself.
syn: censure, rebuke *ant:* acclaim, praise

8. **obsequious** (əb sē′ kwē əs) *adj.* excessively submissive or overly attentive
The waiter's *obsequious* behavior annoyed the patrons at the expensive restaurant.
syn: servile, fawning *ant:* domineering, haughty

9. **obviate** (ŏb′ vē āt) *verb* to prevent; get around
They refused to release the film because they wished to *obviate* a barrage of criticism.
syn: circumvent

10. **offal** (ô′ fəl) *noun* garbage; waste parts
The *offal* from the treatment plant entered the ocean and posed a danger to humans and fish.

11. **olfactory** (ōl făk′ tə rē) *adj.* pertaining to smell
On breezy days, we endured an *olfactory* assault by odors from the landfill.

12. **onerous** (ōn′ ər əs) *adj.* burdensome; heavy; hard to endure
Once the *onerous* car loan was paid off, she would have some breathing room in her budget.

13. **onus** (ō′ nəs) *noun* a burden; responsibility; an obligation
With his father's death, the *onus* of caring for the family fell upon the oldest son.

14. **optimum** (ŏp′ tə mŭm) *adj.* the best; most favorable; ideal
The pilot was waiting for *optimum* conditions before setting out on the dangerous flight.

15. **opulent** (ŏp′ yə lənt) *adj.* rich, luxurious; wealthy
It was obvious from their *opulent* style of living that the stock market decline had not affected them.

Exercise I Words in Context

Fill in the blanks with the correct vocabulary words needed to complete the sentences.

nonentity **optimum** **obfuscate** **opulent**

A. He felt it was the ________________ time to sell his stocks. The market had never been so good, and he wanted the ________________ lifestyle that the profits would afford him. His broker, however, continued to ________________ the situation; and because John had always felt himself a(n) ________________, he had no faith in his own judgment.

nubile **onerous** **olfactory** **offal** **obloquy** **nirvana**

B. The mayor's situation was a(n) ________________ one. He knew something had to be done to find a new landfill, but no one wanted the ________________ in their neighborhood. His suggestion of a trash-to-steam plant met with the same criticism. "Either one," said his critics, "would be an attack upon the ________________ senses."

C. "Each of us," the guru said, "must seek and find his own ________________. There is no road map." At this point, a beautiful, ________________ woman walked to the stage. Suddenly, she shouted, "You big fake!" Turning to the audience, she told them of the ________________ that he had heaped on her because she had refused his advances.

obviate **obsequious** **onus** **obdurate** **non sequitur**

D. Some young soldiers do not want the ________________ of command. In fact, if it appears that it will be thrust upon them, they will often pull some dumb stunt in order to ________________ what they consider an intolerable situation.

E. "Sometimes," Paul said, "I hate myself for being so ________________. At work, I am the perfect 'yes man.' But then I go home and totally change. With my family, I am ________________. I will not give an inch. Happiness isn't meant for me," Paul concluded. "I can never be happy."

"Wait," the doctor said. "Let's examine your last statement. It's a(n) ________________. You are presently unhappy and there are things about your behavior that upset you, but you can change and you can be happy."

Exercise II Roots, Prefixes, and Suffixes

Study the entries and answer the questions that follow.

The root *spir* means "breathe."
The root *sum/sumpt* means "take."
The root *stat/stab* means "stand."
The prefix *re–* means "back."
The prefix *con–* means "together, with."
The prefix *in–* means "into."
The prefix *ad–*, which can change to *as*, means "toward."

1. Literally, a *conspiracy* is ____________________, and *respiration* is ____________________; but if you breathe *spirit* into people you ____________________ them, and now they possess ____________________.

2. If you want to know where you stand, you are inquiring about your ____________________. If you are capable of standing firmly on your ground, you are said to have ____________________.

3. Give a literal definition for each of the following:
   consumption
   resumption
   assumption

Exercise III Usage Inferences

Choose the answer that best suits the situation.

1. Choose the best *non sequitur* to follow, "I hate carrots."
   A. I never order them when I go out to eat.
   B. In fact, I hate all things that are orange.
   C. I was seven years old in 2001.
   D. I feel that people should not eat roots.

2. Which job would likely require a person to be the most *obdurate*?
   A. a social worker
   B. a drill sergeant
   C. a computer designer
   D. a chorus teacher

3. Which is the best example of something that is *opulent*?
   A. an autographed baseball
   B. a fast food meal
   C. playing in the World Series
   D. a diamond necklace

Exercise IV Reading Comprehension

Read the selection and answer the questions.

My first instinct is to say that friendship is impossible except between good men. Now I am not going to cut to the bone in my analysis of "good" like the hair-splitters, who may be right, but contribute little to any generally useful purpose, when they deny that anyone is a good man unless he is "sage." So be it; but the sagacity they are talking about is something no human being ever achieved, whereas we ought to consider the quality as it is in the usage of daily life, not as we may imagine it or wish it to be. I shall never admit that Gaius Fabricius, Manius Curius, or Tiberius Coruncanius, whom our ancestors called wise men, were "sages" according to the criteria of these logic-choppers. Let them keep their vague but arrogant term, as long as they admit that the men I have named were good men. But they will not even consent to that compromise; they insist that the term cannot be used except of a "sage." Let us then proceed with the brains God gave us, as they say. Those whose life and conduct is such that they can be counted on to be trustworthy, impartial, courteous, and generous, who are not greedy, lustful, or overbold, but rather steadfast, like the men I just named, are the men whom we ought, in keeping with their reputation, to call good, because they follow, to the limit of human ability, Nature, the best guide to living well. For as far as I can see, we were born into a mutual association, which grows closer with contact, so that fellow-citizens have a higher claim on us than foreigners, and relatives than strangers; for though in the latter cases nature herself has produced the friendship, it still has not a firm base. Now friendship has this advantage over blood relationship: you can have the latter without good will, but not the former. To understand best how potent friendship is, look at it this way: out of the limitless association of mankind, which Nature herself links together, this is a thing so concentrated and focused that the whole of natural affection links together two people, or not many more.

–Cicero

1. The author's main point in this selection is that
   A. natural affection links two people together as friends.
   B. a sage is someone who conducts himself in a worthy manner.
   C. only between good men is a friendship possible.
   D. nature is the best guide to living well.
   E. None of the above are correct.

2. The author states or implies that he believes
   A. the word "good" may be applied only to sages.
   B. the thinking of the philosophers, "logic choppers," lacks God-given common sense.
   C. we ought to call "good" those steadfast men who are trustworthy, generous, etc.
   D. Both A and B are correct.
   E. Both B and C are correct.

3. Regarding philosophers, the author appears to feel
   A. great sympathy.
   B. mild discomfort.
   C. great humor.
   D. rising impatience.
   E. resigned sadness.

4. The author also states or implies
   A. that strangers have less of a claim on our friendship than relatives.
   B. that fellow citizens have a greater claim than foreigners do.
   C. that nature limits the friendships one may have to two or so people.
   D. Both A and B are correct.
   E. A, B, and C are correct.

Lesson Fourteen

1. **orifice** (ôr′ ə fĭs) *noun* mouth; opening
The lost boy was found high in the mountains in the *orifice* of a deserted drain pipe.

2. **orthography** (ôr thŏg′ rə fē) *noun* correct spelling
The teacher said that students would never get good grades in composition unless they learned *orthography*.

3. **paleontology** (pâ lē ən tŏl′ ə jē) *noun* a science dealing with prehistoric life through study of fossils
By using the techniques of *paleontology*, she dated the skeleton at 2000 B.C.

4. **palliate** (păl′ ē āt) *verb* to ease; lessen; soothe
She became a nurse to *palliate* suffering, but all she had done so far was record temperatures.
syn: alleviate, excuse *ant:* intensify, exacerbate

5. **panache** (pə näsh′) *noun* self-confidence; a showy manner
The actor had great *panache*, so his first visit to the late-night talk show didn't make him the least bit nervous.

6. **pandemic** (pân dĕm′ ĭk) *adj.* general; widespread
The World Health Organization has announced that the disease has become *pandemic*.

7. **panegyric** (pân ə jər′ ĭk) *noun* an expression of praise
The ancient Greeks gave *panegyrics* and crowns of ivy in tribute to their heroes.
syn: tribute, extolment *ant:* denunciation

8. **paradigm** (pâr′ ə dīm) *noun* a model, an example
John was always held up to the rest of the class as a *paradigm* of good manners.

9. **parochial** (pə rō′ kē əl) *adj.* local; narrow; limited
Because he had never traveled outside his own town, Jim had a very *parochial* view of life.
syn: provincial, narrow-minded *ant:* universal, catholic

10. **parody** (pâr′ ə dē) *noun* a work that imitates another in a ridiculous manner
Joan's *parody* of the English teacher was funny to everyone but the English teacher.
syn: caricature, burlesque, lampoon

11. **paroxysm** (pâr′ ək sĭz əm) *noun* a sudden outburst; a fit
The class, which had burst out in a *paroxysm* of laughter, stopped as soon as the principal walked into the room.

12. **patent** (pă′ tənt) *adj.* evident or obvious
Randy knew it was a *patent* lie, and he could not understand why everyone didn't see it as such.

13. **peccadillo** (pĕk ə dĭl′ ō) *noun* a minor misdeed or misbehavior
Picking up the tips from the table was just a *peccadillo* in Bill's mind, but a major offense in the minds of the waiters.

14. **pecuniary** (pĭ kyōō′ nē ər ē) *adj.* pertaining to money; financial
Jill found herself in a bad *pecuniary* position at the end of the month when the rent became due.

15. **pedantic** (pə dân′ tĭk) *adj.* tending to show off one's learning
After one year of college, Tom lost all of his friends because of his *pedantic* behavior.

Exercise I Words in Context

Fill in the blanks with the correct vocabulary words needed to complete the sentences.

palliate **orifice** **pedantic** **paleontologist** **panegyric** **pecuniary**

A. Sure, the ________________ was good for his ego, but a raise would have helped ________________ the terrible ________________ position in which John found himself. He could not pay the rent and buy food for his family with promises and praise.

B. The ________________ found the fossil in a(n) ________________ on the hillside, which was exposed after the earthquake. While the story of his find could have been interesting, he related it in such an ________________ manner that people in his audience were bored and confused.

parody **pandemic** **panache** **paroxysm**

C. As the door opened and the young man entered the room, the music suddenly stopped; there was an unusual period of silence as everyone looked at the newcomer. A young man with less ________________ might have waited, but not Ross. Blowing kisses to everyone in the room, he walked up to the hostess and hugged her. The next day in a restaurant, Mark performed a ________________ of Ross's entrance for the amusement of his grandmother. The old lady broke into a ________________ of laughter, and people around the room smiled. But as he continued his performance and the old lady continued her laughing, more people began to laugh. Soon, the laughter was ________________ . Even the waiters and the grouchy cook were laughing.

parochial **orthography** **patent** **peccadillo** **paradigm**

D. The United States is held up as an ________________ of true democracy. Its constitution does not have a(n) ________________, but a universal application.

E. So I said, "Congratulations" to her rather than "Best Wishes." Is that a major crime? Commit one ________________ with some people, and they hate you forever. I would write her an apology, but she would probably complain that my handwriting is atrocious and my ________________ lamentable. But you can catch her in a(n) ________________ lie, and she will laugh it off as a clever joke.

Exercise II Roots, Prefixes, and Suffixes

Study the entries and answer the questions that follow.

The root *vas/vad* means "go."
The root *trud/trus* means "thrust."
The root *verb* means "word."
The prefix *dia–* means "across."
The prefix *ob–* means "against."
The prefix *in–* means "into."
The prefix *ab–* means "away from."
The suffix *–cide* means "killing of."

1. Literally, if you *intrude*, you ____________________, so the word *obtrusion* probably means ____________________. The word *abstruse* comes from the same root but means "hidden or concealed." How do you suppose *abstruse* came to have that definition?

2. List words with the root *vas/vad*.

3. Something taken down word for word is taken down ____________________, while someone who uses many words is said to be ____________________. In the same vein, if you are accused of *verbiage*, you are ____________________; but that is better than being charged with *verbicide*, which literally means ____________________.

4. List some words that begin with the prefix *dia–*.

Exercise III Usage Inferences

Choose the answer that best suits the situation.

1. Which is an example of an *orifice*?
   A. an open mouth
   B. a doctor's scalpel
   C. a broken monitor
   D. a math test

2. Where would you expect to hear a *panegyric*?
   A. over the loudspeaker of a hospital
   B. at a retirement banquet
   C. in a comic play
   D. at a murder trial

3. Which quotation is the best example of a *peccadillo*?
   A. "I couldn't eat that entire steak."
   B. "I couldn't stop myself from speeding."
   C. "My dog needs more training."
   D. "I finally earned enough to take a vacation."

Exercise IV Reading Comprehension

Read the selection and answer the questions.

Trust thyself; every heart vibrates to that iron string. Accept the place that divine providence has found for you, the society of your contemporaries, the connection of events. Great men have always done so, and confided themselves, childlike, to the genius of their age, betraying their perception that the absolutely trustworthy was seated at their heart, working through their hands, predominating in all their being…

Society everywhere is in conspiracy against the manhood of every one of its members. Society is a joint-stock company, in which the members agree, for the better securing of his bread to each shareholder, to surrender the liberty and culture of the eater. The virtue most request is conformity. Self-reliance is its aversion. It loves not realities and creators, but names and customs.

Who so would be a man, must be a nonconformist. He who would gather immortal palms must not be hindered by the name of goodness, but must explore if it be goodness. Nothing is at last sacred but the integrity of your own mind.

–Ralph Waldo Emerson

1. The author's main point is that every individual
   A. must work hard for the common good.
   B. should strive for greatness.
   C. is an explorer who has lost his way.
   D. has to learn to think for himself.
   E. is a part of something greater than himself.

2. The tone of this selection could best be described as one of
   A. hopeless resignation.
   B. passionate urging.
   C. mild condemnation.
   D. patient understanding.
   E. biting sarcasm.

3. The "society is a joint-stock company" metaphor is used to make the point that
   A. life is an economic game.
   B. everyone gives up some of their individual freedom in order for society to function smoothly.
   C. self-reliance must be encouraged to thrive in order for society to survive.
   D. society is generally run by a closed order of men who look to their own interests first.
   E. Both C and D are correct.

4. The author states or implies that
   A. society hates its members to be self reliant.
   B. nonconformity is generally better than conformity for the thinking man.
   C. everyone must learn to trust himself.
   D. each individual has to decide for himself what is goodness; you can't accept someone else's word for it.
   E. All of the above are correct.

Lesson Fifteen

1. **pedestrian** (pə dĕs′ trē ən) *adj.* ordinary or dull
The crowd failed to respond because it was a *pedestrian* speech.
syn: commonplace, mediocre *ant:* imaginative, compelling

2. **pejorative** (pĭ jôr′ə tĭv) *adj.* having a negative effect; insulting
The comedian was known for making *pejorative* comments, which for some reason the audience found funny.
syn: disparaging, derogatory *ant:* complimentary

3. **perdition** (pər dĭsh′ ən) *noun* damnation; ruin; hell
The sermon was about the sins that lead to *perdition*.

4. **perfunctory** (pər funk′ tə rē) *adj.* done without care; in a routine fashion
She greeted her guests in a *perfunctory* manner.
syn: indifferent, offhand *ant:* diligent, attentive

5. **perspicacity** (pûr spĭ kăs′ ĭ tē) *noun* keenness of judgment
His *perspicacity* was what made him such a good president.
syn: acuteness, discernment *ant:* density; vacuousness

6. **peruse** (pə rōōz′) *verb* to read carefully; scrutinize
Bob *peruses* the classified ads every day to try to find a part-time job.

7. **quagmire** (kwăg′ mīr) *noun* a swamp; a difficult or inextricable situation
The war was a political *quagmire* for three U.S. presidents.

8. **quandary** (kwŏn′ drē) *noun* a puzzling situation; a dilemma
Robert was in a *quandary* deciding what his major should be.
syn: predicament

9. **quasi-** (kwä′ zī) *adj.* resembling; seeming; half
Grandfather was in only *quasi*-retirement because he couldn't give up control of the business.

10. **querulous** (kwĕr′ ə ləs) *adj.* complaining; grumbling
The *querulous* child on the plane was making all of the passengers angry.
syn: fretful, peevish *ant:* complacent, satisfied

11. **quiddity** (kwĭ′ dĭ tē) *noun* an essential quality
The *quiddity* of an object or person is that which makes it what it is.

12. **raiment** (rā′ mənt) *noun* clothing; garments
The royal *raiment* of the princess is copied by the fashion industry for the department store market.

13. **rakish** (rāk′ ĭsh) *adj.* carefree; dashing; jaunty
His hat was on the back of his head and set at a *rakish* angle.

14. **ratiocinate** (ră′ shē ō sən āt) *verb* to reason; to think
Because alcohol had dulled his mind, he was no longer able to *ratiocinate* clearly.

15. **rationalize** (răsh′ ə nəl īz) *verb* to make an excuse for
The boy tried to *rationalize* his absence from school.
syn: justify

Exercise I Words in Context

Fill in the blanks with the correct vocabulary words needed to complete the sentences.

rakish **raiment** **peruse** **perspicacity** **pedestrian**

A. As a young woman, my mother would ________________ the fashion magazines looking for inexpensive clothing tips. She knew her ________________ could never equal the expensive designer clothes, but she had a ________________ about herself and her talents. By putting a feather in her hat at a ________________ angle, she could turn a ________________ -looking hat into a style statement.

quiddity **quasi** **quagmire** **pejorative** **querulous** **perdition**

B. The professor continued, "That which makes a thing what it is, is its essence; therefore, man's ________________ is his eternal spirit or soul. So, if you accept that," he concluded, "it follows that a Superior Being could consign a soul to eternal ________________."

C. As they filed out of the room, she heard a few ________________ comments. "Well, you can't please everyone," she thought. "Office politics," she reasoned, "can be a dangerous ________________." She had been appointed acting manager, but she still had to work in her old position with the rest of the crew. This ________________ -leadership role was so stressful that it began causing problems at home. She became short-tempered with her family who told her that the pressure was turning her into a ________________ nag.

rationalize **perfunctory** **ratiocinate** **quandary**

D. Let's not argue. We will sit down and calmly discuss the problem. Let us ________________ together, and between two heads we might find a solution that neither of us could come up with alone. But let us not waste time. There is no need to ________________ our past mistakes. Mistakes were made by everyone. Let us put that behind us and go on from here.

E. The invitation to the party put Mary into a ________________. Was the invitation ________________, or had she finally been accepted into the social group?

Exercise II Roots, Prefixes, and Suffixes

Study the entries and answer the questions that follow.

The root *vinc/vict* means "conquer."
The root *viv/vit* means "live."
The root *neo* means "new."
The root *volu/volut* means "roll," "turn."
The prefix *in–* means "not."
The prefix *re–* means "back."

1. Someone who is *invincible* is ____________________, but someone who conquers another is the ________________.

2. Give the literal meaning of the following:
vivid
vivacity
revitalize
vital
vivacious

3. The prefix *neo–* in the term *Neo-Nazi* refers to the group's ____________________ ____________________________________, while a *neophyte* at something is a ________________.

4. List words that contain the root *volv/volut*.

Exercise III Usage Inferences

Choose the answer that best suits the situation.

1. Which of the following observations is likely to be considered the most *pejorative*?
   A. He ate enough pie for three people.
   B. He seems to have a healthy appetite.
   C. He should avoid eating junk food.
   D. He eats as fast as he can.

2. Which is the best example of someone *perusing* something?
   A. An investigator studies a report for clues to a crime.
   B. A patient flips through a magazine in a doctor's waiting room.
   C. A rancher rides out to check on his cattle.
   D. Someone reads a novel before going to bed at night.

3. Which situation is most likely to be referred to as a serious *quagmire*?
   A. A company buys farm land to build a factory on, but forgets to file the appropriate legal documents.
   B. A sunken pirate ship is salvaged according to international salvage rules.
   C. The delivery of urgent medical supplies is slowed down because of the complicated forms required to mail them.
   D. A library buys a book that is regarded as offensive to some people in the community.

Exercise IV Reading Comprehension

Read the selection and answer the questions.

#20 For a long time we must read only the best authors, the ones least likely to let us down. We must read carefully, taking almost as much pains as if we were copying it down; and it is not of parts of the work only that we must do our close reading; the book must be read all the way through, and then taken up again from the beginning, especially speeches, whose virtues are often deliberately concealed....

#24 The reader ought not to be too ready to believe that everything the best authors have said is in every way perfect. They slip sometimes, and stagger beneath their burden; they indulge their fancy; they sometimes relax and grow weary. Cicero thought that Demosthenes sometimes nodded; Horace thought the same of Homer himself.

#25 For though they are the best, they are still men, and those who elevate whatever they find in them into a law of language may imitate the inferior parts (which is quite easy) and congratulate themselves that they are fair copies, if they succeed in imitating the shortcomings of the great.

#26 Still, critical judgments about men as important as these should be made with balance and breadth of view; otherwise we may fall into the common error of condemning what we do not understand. But if the reader must miss the mean one way or the other, I should rather have him indiscriminate in his likes, than in his dislikes.

–*Quintilian*

1. The author states or implies that
   A. some books should be read more than once.
   B. we should have priorities in what we read.
   C. we must read everything critically.
   D. Both A and B are correct.
   E. A, B, and C are correct.

2. Something to consider when reading is that
   A. the great authors do not make mistakes.
   B. we have to be careful in criticizing what we do not understand because it might be our lack of understanding, not the writer's.
   C. we have to read even the great authors critically.
   D. Both A and B are correct.
   E. Both B and C are correct.

3. In paragraph #25, the author's main point is that
   A. we must guard against copying the weakest part of the great writers.
   B. the best writers are easily imitated.
   C. we must not congratulate ourselves on knowing the laws of language if we have only read easy writers.
   D. to write like the great authors is our goal.
   E. we must write in our own style, not anyone else's style, even that of the great ones.

4. The last sentence in #26 means that
   A. if we are diligent, our judgment will always be right on the mark.
   B. even though diligent, we will sometimes make an error in judgment about the great authors.
   C. if we make an error in judgment about the great authors, he hopes that we are too accepting of them rather than too critical.
   D. if we make an error in judgment about the great authors, he hopes that we are too critical rather than too accepting.
   E. we discriminate between the good and the bad authors.

Lesson Sixteen

1. **rebuke** (rĭ byōōk′) *verb* to scold; blame
The professor *rebuked* his students for doing poorly on the exam.
syn: admonish, reprimand *ant:* praise, laud

2. **recant** (rĭ kănt′) *verb* to withdraw or disavow a statement or opinion
The suspect *recanted* his confession, so the police had to release him.

3. **recapitulate** (rē kə pĭch′ ə lāt) *verb* to summarize; repeat briefly
Television reporters always *recapitulate* presidential news conferences, as if the audience were incapable of understanding what had been said.

4. **recoil** (rĭ koil′) *verb* to retreat; draw back
At the harsh words, the girl *recoiled* as if she had been struck.

5. **recondite** (rĕ′ kən dīt) *adj.* difficult to understand; profound
His argument was so *recondite* that only a few of the students could follow it.

6. **recreant** (rĕk′ rē ənt) *noun* a coward; traitor
Benedict Arnold was a *recreant,* and history treated him just as he deserved.

7. **rectify** (rĕk′ tə fī) *verb* to correct; make right
Sometimes, it's too late to *rectify* our mistakes.

8. **redolent** (rĕd′ ə lənt) *adj.* having a pleasant odor; suggestive or evocative
The new fabric softener is advertised as being *redolent* of a spring day.

9. **redundant** (rĭ dŭn′ dənt) *adj.* repetitious; using more words than needed
Saying that a person is a rich millionaire is *redundant.*
syn: wordy, excessive, superfluous, unnecessary *ant:* essential

10. **regale** (rĭ gāl′) *verb* to delight with something pleasing or amusing
John *regaled* the crowd for hours with his stories of Scotland.

11. **regress** (rĭ grĕs′) *verb* to move in a backward direction
If he took the job they offered, Tim felt that he might *regress* rather than move forward.

12. **sacrosanct** (săk′ rō sănkt) *adj.* extremely holy
The detective's orders were to investigate everyone; no person was so *sacrosanct* that he or she was above suspicion.

13. **sadistic** (sə dĭs′ tĭk) *adj.* deriving pleasure from inflicting pain on others
Donna took *sadistic* pleasure in tormenting her little sister.

14. **sagacious** (sə gā′ shəs) *adj.* wise; having keen perception and sound judgement
The *sagacious* old man always had the answers to moral problems.
syn: shrewd, intelligent *ant:* obtuse, fatuous

15. **salacious** (sə lā′ shəs) *adj.* obscene; lusty
The minister denounced the movie because of its *salacious* nature.
syn: lecherous *ant:* chaste

Exercise I Words in Context

Fill in the blanks with the correct vocabulary words needed to complete the sentences.

recanted **recapitulate** **sagacious** **salacious** **rebuked**

A. During the trial, the defense lawyer made an issue of the fact that his client had ________________ the confession he had made to the police and argued that it not be allowed into the court record. After being ________________ by the angry judge, the lawyer tried once again in his summation to ________________ his defense.

B. English is a difficult language to learn. The word ________________ means "obscene," and the word ________________ means "wise." The change in only one letter makes a big difference.

recoiled **recondite** **rectify** **redundant**

C. The lawyer presented a very ________________ argument, and some of the members of the jury had a hard time following it. In the end, he had tried to excuse the drug company from any liability, but the jury decided that the company did make a big mistake and now must ________________ the wrong it had done. When the award was brought in, however, it was so large that the defense lawyer ________________ in horror. "Twenty million dollars," he said. "Twenty million," he repeated again and again, quite unaware of how ________________ he was being.

regressive **sadistic** **recreant** **sacrosanct** **regale** **redolent**

D. My grandfather had lived in the West when he was young. During the summer, in the quiet of dusk, when the air was ________________ with cooking smells, mixed with the scent of freshly cut grass, my grandfather would ________________ my friend and me with tales of the Old West. One of his favorite stories recounted the life of the notorious outlaw, Jesse James, and the ________________ who shot him, Bob Ford.

E. It did not take the jury long to bring a guilty verdict in the case of the ________________ criminal.

F. "The policy you propose," said the new university president, "is not progressive; in fact, it is ________________. If we are to have a strong and vital university, we must examine everything. No department is so ________________ that it is exempt from scrutiny."

Exercise II Roots, Prefixes, and Suffixes

Study the entries and answer the questions that follow.

The root *vac* means "empty."
The root *tort/tors* means "twist."
The root *string/strict* means "bind," "draw," "close."
The root *somn* means "sleep."
The root *ambula* means "walk."
The prefix *e–* means "out of."
The prefix *con–* means "together."
The prefix *re–* means "back."
The prefix *in–* means "not."

1. If someone calls you *vacuous*, they are implying that ________________. Literally, *evacuate* means ________________.

2. Give the literal meaning for the following:
   torture
   contortion
   torsion

3. Another word for *strict* or *harsh* is ________________. In this regard, then, the word *stricture* refers to ________________; and the word *restriction* refers to ________________.

4. The condition of not being able to sleep is called ________________, so the word that means "drowsy or sleeping" is ________________. If you walk in your sleep, you have ________________, so something that is *somniferous* must mean ________________.

Exercise III Usage Inferences

Choose the answer that best suits the situation.

1. Who would be the most deserving of a *rebuke*?
   A. an artist who deliberately paints an ugly painting
   B. a referee who bets on the outcome of basketball games
   C. a general who gives an order to advance
   D. an ice skater who never falls during competition

2. Which situation is most likely to be described as *recondite*?
   A. a play about death
   B. a game of chess
   C. a lecture on money
   D. a movie about fires

Exercise IV Reading Comprehension

Read the selection and answer the questions.

What are the great faults of conversation? Want of ideas, want of words, want of manners are the principal ones, I suppose you think. I don't doubt it, but I will tell you what I have found spoil more good talks than anything else. Long arguments on special points between people who differ on the fundamental principles upon which these points depend. No men can have satisfactory relations with each other until they have agreed on certain points of belief not to be disturbed in ordinary conversation, and unless they have sense enough to trace the secondary questions depending upon these ultimate beliefs to their source. In short, just as a written constitution is essential to the best social order, so a code of finalities is a necessary condition of profitable talk between two persons. Talking is like playing on the harp; there is as much in laying the hand on the strings to stop their vibrations as in twanging them to bring out their music.

–Oliver Wendell Holmes

1. In this selection, the author's main point is that
   A. there are three great faults of conversation.
   B. people have few ideas, so they have little to talk about.
   C. talk is the music of the soul.
   D. good conversation requires people to agree on basic points.
   E. Both B and C are correct.

2. The author says that in his mind, the greatest fault of conversation is
   A. lack of ideas.
   B. lack of words.
   C. lack of manners.
   D. All of the above are correct.
   E. None of the above are correct.

3. The author compares the constitution (e.g., of a country) to
   A. nature.
   B. guidelines for a conversation.
   C. music.
   D. good social older.
   E. lack of manners.

4. In the last sentence, the author uses the metaphor of the harp to make the point that
   A. good conversation and good music both involve the use of the hands.
   B. conversation, like music, should not get loud or heated.
   C. knowing when to stop talking is as important as knowing when to talk.
   D. Both A and B are correct.
   E. A, B, and C are correct.

Lesson Seventeen

VOCABULARY *for the* College Bound

1. **salient** (sā′ lē ənt) *adj.* significant; conspicuous; standing out from the rest
   The *salient* facts of the case finally came to light during the eyewitness account.

2. **salutary** (săl′ yə tĕr ē) *adj.* healthful; wholesome
   The country air had a *salutary* influence on the child's chronic cough.
   syn: beneficial *ant:* pernicious

3. **sang-froid** (sän fwa′) *noun* calmness; composure or cool self-possession
   Even though the heckler continued to harass him, the speaker kept his *sang-froid.*
   syn: aplomb *ant:* uneasiness, perturbation

4. **sanguine** (săng′ wĭn) *adj.* cheerful; optimistic
   Sally's *sanguine* personality made everyone in her company pleased to be with her.

5. **sapient** (sā′ pē ənt) *adj.* wise; full of knowledge
   Although a *sapient* man, he pays little attention to worldly concerns.
   syn: sagacious *ant:* fatuous, inane

6. **saturnine** (săt′ ər nīn) *adj.* gloomy; sluggish
   The host's *saturnine* attitude caused the party to end early.
   syn: sullen, morose *ant:* genial

7. **savant** (sə vänt′) *noun* a person of extensive learning; an eminent scholar
   Einstein was a *savant* who will always be remembered for $E = mc^2$.

8. **scintillate** (sĭn′ tĭl āt) *verb* to sparkle; twinkle; to shine intellectually
   The lights *scintillated* throughout the otherwise drab room.

9. **scurrilous** (skûr′ ə ləs) *adj.* coarsely abusive; vulgar
   Blackbeard the pirate and his men would never have been accepted into society because of their *scurrilous* behavior.

10. **sedition** (sĭ dĭsh′ ən) *noun* rebellion or resistance against the government
    The Confederate States of America were charged with *sedition* when they left the Union.

11. **sedulous** (sej′ ə ləs) *adj.* hardworking; diligent
    Everyone knew Jason would get ahead in the world because he was *sedulous* in all he undertook.

12. **sentient** (sĕnt′ shē ənt) *adj.* conscious; capable of feeling or perception
    No one knew if the girl in the coma was *sentient*, but they continued to talk to her.

13. **shard** (shärd) *noun* a fragment
The doctor pulled a *shard* of glass from the girl's arm.

14. **shibboleth** (shĭb′ ə ləth) *noun* a slogan; a password
During the war, anyone who failed the *shibboleth* test was immediately imprisoned.

15. **sibilant** (sĭb′ ə lənt) *adj.* making a hissing sound
The Native American guide couldn't see it, but the *sibilant* sounds told him that a snake was in the grass.

Exercise I Words in Context

Fill in the blanks with the correct vocabulary words needed to complete the sentences.

salient **shibboleth** **salutary** **scintillating** **sang-froid** **sedulously**

A. The doctor generally displayed __________________ no matter what news he had to tell his patient. In this instance, however, he could not help but smile as he told the young mother the __________________ effect the new drug had on her sick infant.

B. The party was filled with __________________ conversation. The one __________________ thing the guests had in common was their social class. It was a fund-raiser for a good cause, and the hostess was __________________ soliciting money from the guests. If she could only come up with a catchy __________________ for the evening, she knew it would be a great success.

savant **saturnine** **sanguine** **sapient** **sibilant**

C. Although normally a __________________ individual, today Albert was depressed. He had just had a conversation with his grandfather, a __________________ old man who had made all his money speculating in stocks. As soon as Albert walked in the door, his wife Vera knew something was wrong from the __________________ expression on his face.

D. Upon hearing the __________________ sound, Russ knew there was a snake in the tent. Slowly, he looked around. Although he had spent the last ten years teaching at a college, he was not a mere __________________ whose knowledge of snakes was limited to what he had read in books. Russ had had a great deal of practical experience with snakes, and now he was thankful for that.

sedition **sentient** **scurrilous** **shard**

E. Walking to the table, the lawyer picked up a __________________ of glass. "It was," he said, "with a piece of glass much like this one, that Raymond Wilson slashed Betty Wilson's face." With this, Ray Wilson jumped up and let loose a __________________ barrage of curses that shocked even the hardened judge. "Today," the lawyer shouted, "after six days in a coma, Betty Wilson is finally __________________, but it is no thanks to this man."

F. After several early defeats, troops loyal to the Prime Minister Benghazi finally recaptured the capital, and this broke the back of the rebellion. Its leaders were arrested for __________________.

Exercise II Roots, Prefixes, and Suffixes

Study the entries and answer the questions that follow.

The root *sci* means "know."
The root *pot* means "drink."
The root *reg/rig/rect* means "rule," "govern."
The prefix *hyper–* means "too much."
The prefix *omni–* means "all."
The suffix *–cide* means "killing of."

1. Someone who knows something before it happens is said to be __________________; and someone who knows everything, or all, is __________________.

2. A word meaning "drink," usually applied to any magic drink, is __________________; but anything that is drinkable is __________________, so *potation* must refer to __________________.

3. Another word for *ruler* is __________________, and the word for killing a king is __________________; therefore, a six-letter word ending in "ime," meaning "a system of government," is __________________, and a word meaning "to follow a regular system" (such as exercise) that ends in "en" is __________________.

4. The word *hyperbole* is a figure of speech that refers to __________________. List three other words that use the prefix *hyper–*.

Exercise III Usage Inferences

Choose the answer that best suits the situation.

1. Which newspaper article is Senator Johnson most likely to call *scurrilous*?
   A. an article that reports rumors about Senator Johnson and his wife
   B. an article that reports Senator Johnson's voting record on family issues
   C. an article that reports about Senator Johnson's working vacation to the Caribbean
   D. an article that praises the senator for his work on illegal drugs

2. Which is the best example of the word *sibilant*?
   A. Maria made me angry.
   B. He heard a humming noise.
   C. Spring says summer is soon.
   D. Charlie chose chocolate.

Exercise IV Reading Comprehension

Read the selection and answer the questions.

Cooper's gift in the way of invention was not a rich endowment; but such as it was he liked to work it, and he was pleased with the effects. In his little box of stage-properties he kept six or eight cunning devices, tricks, artifices for his savages and woodsmen to deceive and circumvent each other with, and he was never so happy as when he was working these innocent things and seeing them go. A favorite one was to make a moccasined person tread in the tracks of the moccasined enemy, and thus hide his own trail. Cooper wore out barrels and barrels of moccasins in working that trick. Another stage-property that he pulled out of his box pretty frequently was his broken twig. He prized his broken twig above all the rest of his effects, and worked it the hardest. It is a restful chapter in any book of his when somebody doesn't step on a dry twig and alarm all the reds and whites for two hundred yards around. Every time a Cooper person is in peril, and absolute silence is worth four dollars a minute, he is sure to step on a dry twig. There may be a hundred handier things to step on, but that wouldn't satisfy Cooper. Cooper requires him to turn out and find a dry twig; and if he can't do it, go and borrow one. In fact, the *Leather Stocking Series* ought to have been called the *Broken Twig Series*.

–*Mark Twain*

1. The author states or implies that
   A. Cooper was a great writer.
   B. Cooper had an interesting style.
   C. Cooper overused many of the devices in his novels.
   D. Cooper was a very inventive writer.
   E. Both B and D are correct.

2. This selection may best be described as one of
   A. scathing criticism.
   B. mild praise.
   C. satiric criticism.
   D. uncritical adulation.
   E. bitter denunciation.

3. The author's primary purpose in this selection is to point out that Cooper
   A. was a much overrated writer.
   B. was a gifted, if limited, writer.
   C. used the dry twig device too much.
   D. was not a creative or inventive writer.
   E. did not know much about tracking or woodcraft.

4. The statement, "Cooper's gift in the way of invention was not a rich endowment" is an example of satiric
   A. farce.
   B. hyperbole.
   C. understatement.
   D. guilt by association.
   E. Both A and B are correct.

BOOK C

VOCABULARY *for the* College Bound

Lesson Eighteen

1. **anarchy** (ăn′ ăr kē) *noun* the absence of law and government; chaos
Soon after Macbeth killed Duncan, the rightful king, and took power himself, Scotland descended into *anarchy*.

2. **boycott** (boi′ kät) *verb* to avoid dealing with a company as a protest against it in order to make it alter policies
The Animal Rights group *boycotted* the one manufacturer in the state that continued to test cosmetics on rabbits.

3. **chattel** (chăt′ l) *noun* an item of tangible property that is moveable; a slave
In the Dred Scott case, the Supreme Court ruled that a slave was only property, not a person, and could be considered *chattel*.

4. **conscription** (kän skrĭp′ shən) *noun* compulsory service in the military of a country
To avoid the horrors of *conscription* into the Czar's army, my grandfather escaped from Russia and emigrated to the United States.
syn: draft

5. **filibuster** (fĭl′ ə bəs tər) *noun* a delaying tactic used to prevent voting on legislation occurring
verb to prevent action on a bill or other form of legislation by engaging in lengthy debate or obstruction
One senator can prevent the Senate from acting on a bill if he or she begins a *filibuster* or, in some cases, simply by threatening to begin one.

6. **habeas corpus** (hā′ bē əs kör′ pəs) *noun* a law stating that a person must be brought before a court; Latin for "you should have the body"
Since Josh could not locate the witness he needed to prove his innocence, he requested that the court issue a *habeas corpus* order for her to appear.

7. **laissez faire** (lə′ zā făr) *noun* a doctrine that opposes all but minimal governmental interference in private industry; French for "to let (people) do (as they please)"
To modern economists, there must be a middle ground between complete *laissez faire* and an economic system in which all aspects of industry are controlled.

8. **libertarian** (lĭb ər târ′ ē ən) *noun* a belief or one who believes in less government, near total freedom, and fewer rules
The *Libertarian* Party's candidate in one state won the election and is starting a new policy regarding the income tax; it will be abolished.

9. **multiculturalism** (məl tē kəltch′ ərl ĭz əm) *noun* a combining of various and different cultures into one
New York in the early 1900s could not be considered the city of *multiculturalism* that it is today, since, while there were many culturally distinct neighborhoods, they rarely interacted with one another.

10. **neutrality** (nōō trăl′ ĭ tē) *noun* the quality of being objective; not taking sides, especially in war
Although Miranda tried to have an air of *neutrality* about her, we knew that she definitely preferred one diamond ring to the other.

11. **noblesse oblige** (nō blĕs′ ō blēzh′) *noun* the moral obligation of the rich to act with honor, generosity, and benevolence; French for "nobility obliges"
All the monarch's children believed in the idea of *noblesse oblige*, but none of them understood that a fair society puts many other demands on wealth and power.

12. **purge** (pərj) *noun* a forced evacuation and elimination of a people, especially opponents of the government, from an area
The military government attempted a *purge* of farmers from the villages around the river delta once gold deposits were discovered there.
syn: resettle

13. **Renaissance** (rĕn′ ə zŏns) *noun* the period in European history between 1400 and 1600 approximately, which featured many artistic and intellectual changes; a rebirth
Once the Inquisition had ended, people affected by its horrors expected a *renaissance* of religious tolerance, but, unfortunately, complete freedom of worship did not materialize.

14. **totalitarian** (tō tăl ĭ târ′ ē ən) *adj.* relating to a government that exercises absolute control over its citizens
The *totalitarian* regime focused all its funds on preserving its rule, and it completely ignored the needs of the country's people, who were suffering from a devastating famine.
syn: dictatorial *ant:* democratic

15. **writ** (rĭt) *noun* a written order; a written document issued by a court
The victim's family protested when the governor issued a *writ*, which commuted the prisoner's death sentence and changed it to life imprisonment.

Exercise I Words in Context

Fill in the blanks with the correct vocabulary words needed to complete the sentences.

writ **Renaissance** **noblesse oblige** **purges** **totalitarian**

A. Prior to and even during the ________________ in Europe, there was little assimilation of diverse groups in most societies. People tended to live, work, and congregate in their own groups. This tendency to isolate themselves, however, made it easier for ________________ governments to subject them to ________________. There was rarely a ________________ issued demanding their expulsion—that job was left to the local nobles, who treated peasants very poorly. Many nobles, however, believed in the idea of ________________, and these kind families protected the people in surrounding villages.

multicultural **libertarians** **chattel** **filibuster** **habeas corpus**

B. No one deserves to be treated as ________________, dependent upon the handouts of others. In a complex, varied, ________________ society such as ours, everyone should be treated fairly. The Founding Fathers, many of whom favored small governments and would be considered ________________ today, recognized this necessity, declaring that all men were created equal. Special laws protecting the unjustly accused became part of the Constitution, and its authors made sure to include the right of ________________ in it. However, the implementation of many laws, such as mandated integration and voting rights for women, has been delayed by the use of the ________________, which continued until enough senators recognized the need to stop these tactics and voted to end it.

boycotted **neutrality** **anarchy** **laissez faire** **conscription**

C. The ________________ policies of the government allowed companies that did business with the military to accumulate great wealth while paying very low taxes. During the war in East Asia, the country declared its formal ________________, had no ________________, and was able to sell armaments to all sides, which added to the companies' fortunes. After the war, however, the victor protested the policy of making money through the suffering of others and openly ________________ all weapon sales from that country. This rapid loss of an enormous income had horrible effects on every aspect of society, and near-________________ caused havoc throughout the land.

Exercise II Roots, Prefixes, and Suffixes

Study the entries and answer the questions that follow.

The root *nasc/nas/nat* means "be born."
The suffix *–ism* means "doctrine," "belief,"
"action," or "conduct."
The root *purg* means "cleanse, purify."
The root *neuter/neutr* means "neither (of two)."
The suffix *–ity* means "the condition or quality of being."

1. If you take a medicine to counteract the effect of something, you are ________________ it. Having your pet ________________ eliminates its ability to mate, essentially making it gender ________________.

2. *Socialism* is an economic and political theory advocating government control of the means of production and distribution of goods. List three other words that use the suffix *–ism.*

3. Give the literal meaning for the following:
   nascent
   native
   innate
   purgation
   purgatory

4. Some criminals try to use an ________________ defense to avoid punishment for their crimes. They claim that they did not have the ________________ to control their behavior. In each case, psychiatrists evaluate the defendant's mental ________________ to determine if he or she is truly mentally ill.

Exercise III Usage Inferences

Choose the answer that best suits the situation.

1. Which sentence would most likely be used by someone believing in *noblesse oblige?*
   A. I believe in the concept of the rights of man.
   B. I believe in sharing the wealth of the country.
   C. I believe in helping those less fortunate than I am.
   D. I believe the wealthy earned their money honestly.

2. Which would be the best example of *boycotting* a company?
   A. A rival buys its inventory and sells it at a 50% discount.
   B. You encourage friends to buy its products only at discounted prices.
   C. Customers tell neighbors about its illegal and discriminatory practices.
   D. You do not shop at any of its stores because it uses child labor.

3. Which of the following shows *conscription?*
   A. being forced to join the army
   B. not attending school
   C. failing to get a license
   D. becoming a member of the clergy

Exercise IV Reading Comprehension

Read the selection and answer the questions.

Opposed by so many and such formidable foes, Napoleon appeared not to lose either his courage or his military genius. He disconcerted the allies by the rapidity of his movements, and gained several brilliant successes through these strategies; which, though they did not carry with them any lasting advantage, made his enemies still doubtful of the result. On the 29th of January, Blucher was attacked by Napoleon near Brienne so suddenly that he narrowly escaped being taken prisoner. Negotiations for a peace were, however, commenced at Chatillon early in February, 1814; but the insincerity which marked the conduct of the French commissioners prevented them from coming to any conclusion. Napoleon had at length beaten his enemies into the art of conquering, so that while he was maneuvering in their rear, the Prussians and Austrians made a rush on Paris, which fell almost without resistance, capitulated, and the Senate decreed the imperial crown forfeited, and the Empire fallen. Napoleon abdicated, and Louis XVIII was recalled from exile to ascend the throne of his ancestors. The ex-Emperor had assigned to him the island of Elba as an independent sovereignty, with a pension of two millions francs.…On the 4th of May, 1814, the white banner of the Bourbons replaced the tricolor of Austerlitz, and, on the 30th of the same month, Talleyrand, the real head of the provisional government, signed with the allies a convention, with the view of affording France the benefits of peace before a regular treaty could be prepared.

–Sutherland Menzies

1. According to the passage, who or what was partially responsible for defeating Napoleon?
   A. Blucher
   B. Bourbons
   C. Talleyrand
   D. Prussians
   E. Louis XVIII

2. What sentence conveys the proper meaning of "Napoleon had at length beaten his enemies into the art of conquering..."?
   A. Napoleon had conquered and beaten his enemies.
   B. The art of conquering had been taught to Napoleon's allies.
   C. The art of conquest had been learned by Napoleon.
   D. Napoleon had taught his enemies the art of conquering.
   E. Napoleon's art of conquest had never been learned by his enemies.

3. What is the best meaning of the word *disconcerted*, as it is used in the second sentence?
   A. destroyed
   B. confused
   C. defeated
   D. scattered
   E. encircled

4. Who or what is the "imperial crown"?
   A. Napoleon
   B. the dead king
   C. a law passed by the Senate
   D. Louis XVIII
   E. Paris